RULERS OF INDIA: ALBUQUERQUE

First published 1892
This edition published by Lector House in 2025

ISBN: 978-93-6138-533-9

Lector House LLP
Registered Office: H. No. 96, Block C, Tomar Colony,
Burari, Delhi – 110084, India
info@lectorhouse.com
www.lectorhouse.com

RULERS OF INDIA:
ALBUQUERQUE

HENRY MORSE STEPHENS,
WILLIAM WILSON HUNTER

2025

LECTOR HOUSE LLP

Afonso de Albuquerque. 2°

RULERS OF INDIA: ALBUQUERQUE

BY

H. MORSE STEPHENS

LECTURER ON INDIAN HISTORY AT CAMBRIDGE
AUTHOR OF 'A HISTORY OF THE FRENCH REVOLUTION,'
'THE STORY OF PORTUGAL,' etc.

EDITED BY
SIR WILLIAM WILSON HUNTER, K.C.S.I., C.I.E.
M.A. (OXFORD); LL.D. (CAMBRIDGE)

PREFACE

Affonso de Albuquerque was the first European since Alexander the Great who dreamed of establishing an empire in India, or rather in Asia, governed from Europe. The period in which he fought and ruled in the East is one of entrancing interest and great historical importance, and deserves more attention than it has received from the English people, as the present ruling race in India. Dr. A. C. Burnell, an authority second to none in Indian historical questions, says in his prefatory note to *A Tentative List of Books and some MSS. relating to the History of the Portuguese in India Proper:* 'In the course of twenty years' studies relating to India, I found that the history of the Portuguese had been shamefully neglected.... In attempting to get better information, I found that the true history of the Portuguese in India furnishes most important guidance for the present day, and the assertions commonly made about it are utterly false, especially in regard to the ecclesiastical history.' I purpose, therefore, to give a short list of the more important works on the history of the Portuguese in the East during the sixteenth century, while they were a conquering and a ruling power, in the hope that it may be useful to any one wishing to investigate the subject further than it has been possible for me to do in this volume. I confine myself to the sixteenth century and to books on political history, as I have not the knowledge to classify the numerous works on the history of the Roman Catholic Missions in India, which is closely bound up with the ecclesiastical history of the Portuguese in the East.

Before mentioning books of general history, I must draw attention to the *Commentaries of Albuquerque* on which this volume is chiefly based, as indeed all biographies of the great governor must necessarily be. They were published by his son, Braz de Albuquerque, in 1557, reprinted by him in 1576, and republished in four volumes in 1774. They have been translated into English for the Hakluyt Society by Walter de Gray Birch in four volumes, 1875-1884, and from this translation the quotations in the present volume are taken. The nature and the authority of this most valuable and interesting work are best shown by quoting the first sentence of the compiler's dedication of the second edition to the King of Portugal, Dom Sebastian. 'In the lifetime of the King, Dom João III., your grandfather, I dedicated to Your Highness these Commentaries, which I have collected from the actual originals written by the great Affonso de Albuquerque in the midst of his adventures to the King, Dom Manoel, your great-grandfather.' The *Commentaries* have been for three centuries the one incontestable printed authority for Albuquerque's career. But in 1884 was published the first volume of the *Cartas de Affonso de Albuquerque, seguidas de Documentos que as elucidam,* under the direction of the *Academia Real das Sciencias de Lisboa,* and edited by Raymundo Antonio de Bulhão Pato. This collection includes a large number of despatches to the King, dated February, 1508; October, 1510; April, 1512; August to December, 1512; November, 1513, to January, 1514; October to December, 1514; and September to December, 1515; of which two, dated 1 April, 1512, and 4 December, 1513, are of great importance, and veritable manifestoes of policy. It contains also a more correct version of Albuquerque's last letter to the King than that given in the *Commentaries*. It is to be hoped that the many and serious *lacunæ,* shown by the above dates, will be filled in the long-expected second volume of the *Cartas*.

Turning to the more general authorities on the history of the Portuguese in India in the sixteenth century, it will be well to take them in a rough classification of their importance and authenticity.

João de Barros (1496-1570), for many years treasurer and factor at the India House at Lisbon, published *Asia: dos Feitos que os Portuguezes fizeram no Descobrimento e Conquista dos Mares e Terras do Oriente*. This work is a primary authority, as the writer had access to all documents, and was the recognised historian of the events he described during his lifetime. It is written in imitation of Livy, and is divided into Decades. The first Decade was published in 1552, the second in 1555, the third in 1563, and the fourth after his death in 1615, and it carries the history down to 1539. The best edition is that in nine volumes, Lisbon, 1777-78. A German translation by Dietrich Wilhelm Soltau was published in five volumes at Brunswick, 1821, and it has been largely borrowed from by succeeding writers.

Diogo do Couto (1542-1616) was long employed in India, and had access to documents. He continued the work of Barros in the same style. His first Decade overlaps Barros, and his history goes from 1526 to 1600. The best edition is that published as a continuation of Barros, in fifteen volumes, Lisbon, 1778-1787.

Gaspar Correa (died at Goa between 1561 and 1583) went to India in 1514 and was Secretary to Albuquerque. His *Lendas da India* treat the history of the Portuguese from 1497 to 1549, and was published for the first time at Lisbon, four volumes, 1858-64. His chronology throughout differs much from Barros, and a critical comparison between them is much needed. A portion of this work has been translated by Lord Stanley of Alderley, for the Hakluyt Society, under the title of *The Three Voyages of Vasco da Gama, and his Viceroyalty,* 1869.

Fernão Lopes de Castanheda (died 1559) travelled much in India. He published his *Historia do Descobrimento e Conquista da India pelos Portuguezes,* which covers from 1497 to 1549, in 1551-1561, and is therefore anterior to Barros in date of publication.

Damião de Goes (died 1573), *Commentarius Rerum gestarum in India citra Gangem a Lusitanis,* Louvain, 1539, is a small but early work.

These are primary authorities, but the following chronicles also contain some useful information:

Damião de Goes (died 1573), *Chronica do felicissimo Rey Dom Manoel,* Lisbon, 1566, 1567.

Jeronymo Osorio (died 1580), *De Rebus Emmanuelis Regis,* Lisbon, 1571.

The historians of subsequent centuries simply use, with more or less judgment, the materials provided for them by the historians mentioned above for the sixteenth century, and with one exception are of no value. The one exception is:

Manoel de Faria e Sousa, who in his *Asia Portugueza,* three volumes, Lisbon, 1666-75, made use of good MS. materials.

The purely secondary historians, who in spite of their reputation are better left unread, are: Giovanni Pietro Maffei, *Historiarum Indicarum Libri XVI,* Florence, 1588; Antonio de San Roman, *Historia General de la India Oriental,* Valladolid, 1603; Joseph François Lafitau, *Histoire des Découvertes et des Conquêtes des Portugais dans le Nouveau Monde,* Paris, 1733.

Os Portuguezes em Africa, Asia, America e Oceania, published in Lisbon in 1849, is a lively summary of the best authorities.

In modern times the scientific historical spirit has developed greatly in Portugal, under the influence of the great historian Alexandre Herculano de Carvalho e Araujo, and the publication of documents has taken the place of the publication of historical summaries. Among these ranks first the *Collecção de Monumentos ineditos para a Historia das Conquistas dos Portuguezes em Africa, Asia e America,* a series of which any nation might be proud, and of which the *Cartas de Albuquerque* already described forms a part. It is published under the superintendence of the *Academia Real das Sciencias* of Lisbon, which also brought out, in 1868, *Subsidios para a Historia da India Portugueza,* containing three valuable early documents, edited by Rodrigo José de Lima Felner. Intelligent and thoroughly scientific articles have also appeared in the Portuguese periodicals, especially in the *Annaes Maritimos* in 1840-44, and in the *Annaes das Sciencias e Letteras,* in which was published Senhor Lopes de Mendonça's article on Dom Francisco de Almeida. Mention should also be made of two books published in India, *Contributions to the Study of Indo-Portuguese Numismatics,* by J. Gerson da Cunha, Bombay, 1880, an interesting pamphlet on a fascinating subject, and *An Historical and Archæological Sketch of the City of Goa,* by José Nicolau da Fonseca, Bombay, 1878, a most carefully compiled volume.

In conclusion I must express my gratitude to the editor of the series for much kindly advice and assistance, to Mr. E. J. Wade of the India Office Library, who has been my ever ready helper, and to Mr. T. Fisher Unwin for giving the plate of the portrait of Albuquerque, which appears as a frontispiece.

H.M.S.

Map of 19th century British India.

Map of 19th century British India. (Enlarged - Left)

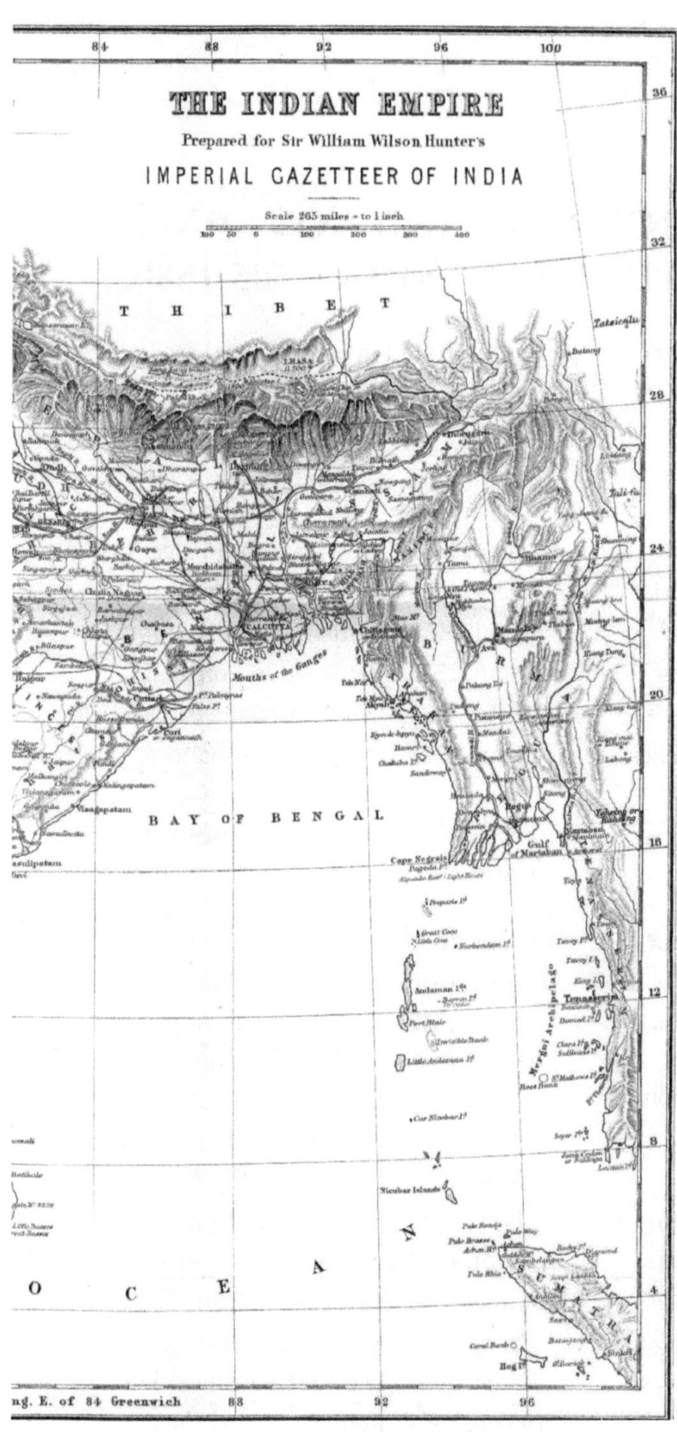

Map of 19th century British India. (Enlarged - Right)

LIST OF VICEROYS AND GOVERNORS OF PORTUGUESE INDIA, 1505-1580.

The names of Viceroys are printed in small capitals.

	Assumed Office.	
DOM FRANCISCO DE ALMEIDA	12 Sept. 1505	Killed by Kaffirs at Saldanha Bay, 1 March, 1510.
Affonso de Albuquerque	4 Nov. 1509	Died off Goa, 16 Dec. 1515.
Lopo Soares de Albergaria	8 Sept. 1515	Returned to Portugal.
Diogo Lopes de Sequeira	8 Sept. 1518	Returned to Portugal.
Dom Duarte de Menezes	22 Jan. 1522	Returned to Portugal.
DOM VASCO DA GAMA	5 Sept. 1524	Died at Cochin, 24 Dec. 1524.
Dom Henrique de Menezes	17 Jan. 1525	Died at Cannanore, 21 Feb. 1526.
Lopo Vaz de Sam Paio	Feb. 1526	Returned to Portugal.
Nuno da Cunha	18 Nov. 1529	Died at sea on his way to Portugal.
DOM GARCIA DE NORONHA	14 Sept. 1538	Died at Goa, 3 April, 1540.
Dom Estevão da Gama	3 April, 1540	Returned to Portugal.
Martim Affonso de Sousa	8 May, 1542	Returned to Portugal.
DOM JOÃO DE CASTRO (Viceroy for 14 days only)	10 Sept. 1545	Died at Goa, 6 June, 1548.
Garcia de Sá	6 June, 1548	Died at Goa, 13 June, 1549.
Jorge Cabral	13 June, 1549	Returned to Portugal.
DOM AFFONSO DE NORONHA	Nov. 1550	Returned to Portugal.
DOM PEDRO MASCARENHAS	23 Sept. 1554	Died at Goa, 16 June, 1555.
Francisco Barreto	16 June, 1555	Returned to Portugal.
DOM CONSTANTINO DE BRAGANZA	8 Sept. 1558	Returned to Portugal.
DOM FRANCISCO DE COUTINHO	7 Sept. 1561	Died at Goa, 9 Feb. 1564.
João de Mendonça	19 Feb. 1564	Returned to Portugal.

Dom Antão de Noronha	3 Sept. 1564	Died at sea on his way to Portugal.
Dom Luis de Athaide	10 Sept. 1568	Returned to Portugal.
Dom Antonio de Noronha	6 Sept. 1571	Returned to Portugal.
Antonio Moniz Barreto	9 Dec. 1573	Returned to Portugal.
Dom Diogo de Menezes	Sept. 1576	Returned to Portugal.
Dom Luis de Athaide *(second time)*	31 Aug. 1578	Died at Goa, 10 March, 1581.

CONTENTS

NOTE

The orthography of proper names follows the system adopted by the Indian Government for the *Imperial Gazetteer of India*. That system, while adhering to the popular spelling of very well-known places, such as Punjab, Poona, Deccan, &c., employs in all other cases the vowels with the following uniform sounds:—

a, as in wom*a*n: *á*, as in l*a*nd: *i*, as in pol*i*ce: *í*, as in intr*i*gue: *o*, as in c*o*ld: *u*, as in b*u*ll: *ú*, as in r*u*le.

ALBUQUERQUE

CHAPTER I

THE PREDECESSORS OF ALBUQUERQUE

The period of the growth and domination of the Portuguese power in India is marked by many deeds of bloodshed and by many feats of heroism; it is illustrated by many great names, among which the greatest without doubt is that of Affonso de Albuquerque. But the general and administrator, to whom his countrymen have given the well-deserved title of *The Great,* was only one of many famous heroes, and it is impossible to understand the greatness of his conceptions and of his deeds without having some idea of the general history of the Portuguese in India.

The importance to Europe of the successful establishment of the Portuguese in the East was manifested in two widely different directions. On the one hand, it checked the rapid advance of Muhammadanism as represented by the Turks. In the sixteenth century the advance of the Turks was still a terror to Europe; Popes still found it necessary to preach the necessity of a new Crusade; the kings of Christendom occasionally forgot their own feuds to unite against the common enemy of the Christian religion; and the Turks were then a progressive and a conquering and not, as they are now, a decaying power. It was at this epoch of advancing Muhammadanism that the Portuguese struck a great blow at Moslem influence in Asia which tended to check its progress in Europe.

Of equal importance to this great service to the cause of humanity was the fact that the Portuguese by establishing themselves in Asia introduced Western ideas into the Eastern world, and paved the way for that close connection which now subsists between the nations of the East and of the West. That connection was in its origin commercial, but other results have followed, and the influence of Asia upon Europe and of Europe upon Asia has extended indefinitely into all departments of human knowledge and of human endeavour.

A wide contrast must be drawn between the Portuguese connection with Asia and between the English and Spanish connection with America. In the latter case the exploring and conquering Europeans had to deal with savage tribes, and in many instances with an uncultivated country; in the former the Portuguese found themselves confronted with a civilisation older than that of Europe, with men more highly educated and more deeply learned than their own priests and men of letters, and with religions and customs and institutions whose wisdom equalled their antiquity.

The India which was reached by Vasco da Gama, and with which the Portuguese monopolised the direct communication for more than a century, was very different to the India with which the Dutch and English merchants sought concessions to trade. The power of the Muhammadans in India was not yet concentrated in the hands of the great Mughals; there were Moslem kingdoms in the North of India and in the Deccan, but the South had not yet felt the heavy hand of Musalman conquerors, and the Hindu Rájá of Vijayanagar or Narsingha was the most powerful potentate in the South of India. The monarchs and chieftains whom the Portuguese first encountered were Hindus. Muhammadan merchants indeed controlled the commerce of their dominions, but they had no share in the government; and one of the ruling and military classes consisted, on the Malabar coast, where the Portuguese first touched, of Nestorian Christians.

The concentration of all commerce in the hands of the believers in the Prophet was not favourably regarded by the wisest of the Hindu rulers, who were therefore inclined to heartily welcome any competitors for their trade. The condition of the Malabar coast at the time of the arrival of the Portuguese was particularly favourable to the Portuguese endeavours, and, had they been inspired with nineteenth-century instead of with sixteenth-century ideas of religion and morality, a prosperous and peaceful commerce might easily have sprung up between the East and the West.

But if the India which Vasco da Gama reached was favourably inclined to open relations with the nation to which he belonged, Portugal was also at that time singularly well fitted by circumstances to send forth men of daring and enterprise to undertake the task. The Portuguese nation had grown strong and warlike from its constant conflict with the Moors in the Peninsula, and the country attained its European limits in 1263. Since that time it had become both rich and populous, and a succession of internal troubles had led to the establishment of a famous dynasty upon the throne of Portugal.

King John I, the founder of the house of Aviz, and surnamed *The Great,* had won his throne by preserving the independence of the Portuguese nation against the power of Castile, with the help of the English, and rested his foreign policy upon a close friendship with the English nation. He married an English princess, a daughter of John of Gaunt, and by her became the father of five sons, whose valour and talents were famous throughout Europe. There being no more Moors to fight in the Peninsula, the Portuguese, led by their gallant princes, went to fight Moors in Morocco. The duty of fighting Moors had from their history sunk deep into the hearts of the Portuguese people. Their history had been one long struggle with Muhammadans, and the Christian religion had therefore taken with them a fiercer and more warlike complexion than in any other country. This feeling was fostered by King Affonso V, the grandson of John the Great, who ruled in Portugal from 1438 to 1481, and who, from his many expeditions to Morocco, obtained the surname of *The African*. His perpetual wars both with the Spaniards and the Moors continued to keep the Portuguese a nation of soldiers; and when the conquest of the East demanded the services of daring men, there was never any lack of soldiers to go upon the most distant expeditions. It was fortunate for the great enterprises of Vasco da Gama and of Affonso de Albuquerque that they had no difficulty in obtaining plenty of brave and experienced warriors; but it is to be deplored that these soldiers were possessed by a spirit of fanaticism against the religion of Islám which stained their victories with cruel deeds. Such fanaticism is indeed deplorable, but considering the past history of the Portuguese nation and the century in which they performed their great feats of arms it was not unnatural.

Commerce with the East sprang up in Europe with civilisation. As soon as any nation became rich it began to desire luxuries which could not be procured at home. The Romans in the days of their greatness knew of the products of Asia, and attained them at a great price. Throughout the Middle Ages the commodities of Asia were known and valued, and as civilisation progressed and Europe emerged from barbarism the demand for pepper and ginger, for spices and silks and brocades increased.

The original trade routes for the products of India were overland. The goods were borne in caravans from the North-West frontier of India across Persia to Aleppo and thence by ship to Italy and to whatever other country was rich enough to purchase them. But after the growth of Muhammadanism and of the power of the Turks, the caravan routes across Central Asia became unsafe. Two new routes then came into use, the one by the Persian Gulf, and the other by the Red Sea. Goods which went by the Persian Gulf were carried overland to Aleppo and other ports in the Levant; goods that went by the Red Sea were carried across Egypt from Suez to Alexandria. From these two entrepôts of Eastern and especially of Indian trade the articles of commerce were fetched by Venetian ships, and from Venice were distributed throughout Europe.

In the days of the Renaissance the products of the East passed through the hands of Muhammadan merchants from India to the Mediterranean, and the large profits they made were commensurate with the risks they undertook. With the rapid growth of civilisation the value of this trade became enormous: every city through which it passed was enriched; Venice became the wealthiest State in Europe; and the cost of all Indian luxuries and spices was extravagantly high.

All wise kings envied the prosperity of Venice, and schemed to secure a share of the Eastern trade for their subjects. Mention has been made of the five illustrious princes, the sons of John the Great and Eleanor of Lancaster. One of them is known in history as Prince Henry the Navigator. This prince devoted his life to the discovery of a direct sea route from Portugal to India. He established himself on the promontory of Sines, and collected around him the most learned geographers and mathematicians of the age. With them he discussed the probability of its being possible to sail round the continent of Africa and thus reach India. Year after year he sent forth expeditions to explore the African coast. Many and important discoveries were made by his navigators, and a generation of skilful pilots and adventurous sailors was formed by his wise encouragement.

Among the earliest discoveries by the sailors of Prince Henry were the islands of Madeira and the Azores, and at the time of his death, in 1460, the Portuguese navigators had learned the way past the River Senegal. What Prince Henry the Navigator began was continued by the enterprise of the Portuguese merchants. These men were not actuated by the high aims of Prince Henry; they were rather inclined to mock at his belief in the existence of a direct sea route to India. But with his discoveries along the African coast began the slave trade. It was found to be excessively profitable to import negroes from the Guinea coast, and the Portuguese captains and pilots soon mastered the difficulties of the navigation of the North-West shoulder of Africa from the frequent voyages which they made in search of slaves.

In 1481 King John II succeeded his father Affonso V upon the throne of Portugal. He was one of the wisest monarchs of his age, and was surnamed by his people John 'the Perfect.' By his internal policy he, like his contemporaries Louis XI of France and Henry VII of England, broke the power of his nobility. His people aided him, for they were wearied of the pressure of feudalism, and he concentrated the whole power of the realm in his own hands. He took up the projects which had been left untouched since the death of his great-uncle, Prince Henry the Navigator. The dream of his life was to find the direct sea route to India. To achieve this end he collected at his Court all the learned men he could attract; he improved the methods of shipbuilding, and began to build full-decked ships of 100 tons; he did much to perfect the knowledge of navigation; and exploration became his favourite hobby.

John II dismissed Columbus as a visionary, and thus left it to Spain to acquire the fame and the profit of discovering the new world of America. But he was diligent in making enquiries, with regard to the East. He sent two of his equerries, João Peres de Covilhão and Affonso de Paiva, overland to India, and the former of these two travellers accompanied the caravans to the East and visited the Malabar coast. He was refused a passage from Calicut to Africa by the jealous Muhammadan merchants, but he managed to find his way through Arabia to Abyssinia, where he died. More important than these overland expeditions were those which John II sent on the tracks of Prince Henry's sailors along the African coast. One of his captains, Diogo Cão or Cam, discovered the Congo in 1484, and in 1486 Bartholomeu Dias and João Infante for the first time doubled the Cape of Good Hope and reached Algoa Bay. John II, like Prince Henry, was fated not to see the fulfilment of his dearest hopes; but he it was who designed the expedition which, under the command of Vasco da Gama, reached India, and who trained the great captains and governors who were to make illustrious with their valour the name of the Portuguese in Asiatic seas.

It was in the month of July, 1497, that a fleet of three ships was placed under the command of Vasco da Gama to follow the route taken by Bartholomeu Dias and find the way to India. Vasco da Gama was the third son of Estevão da Gama, who is said to have been the captain nominated by John II for the command of the expedition. Other accounts give to King Emmanuel, the successor of John II, the credit of choosing the successful admiral. Whoever selected him made a wise choice, for Vasco da Gama showed himself during his eventful voyage possessed of the highest qualities of constancy and daring. The two ships which sailed under his command, in addition to his own, were placed under his elder brother Paulo da Gama and his intimate friend Nicolas Coelho, who proved themselves worthy of their chief. The fleet, of which the crews did not number more than 160 men, nor the tonnage of any ship more than 120 tons, experienced terrific storms in doubling the Cape of Good Hope, but eventually Vasco da Gama struck the South-East coast of Africa. He met with opposition from the rulers of Mozambique and Quiloa (Kilwa), where he first touched, and it was only with the greatest difficulty that he suppressed an incipient mutiny among his sailors.

In April, 1498, he reached Melinda, a port situated 200 miles to the north of Zanzibar, where he was kindly received by the ruling chief. The passage across the Indian Ocean was well known to the navigators of the South-East coast of Africa, for there was a considerable amount of trade conducted between the two localities which was almost entirely controlled by Muhammadans. At Melinda, Vasco da Gama was able to obtain experienced pilots, and after a stay there of one month according to most authorities, and of three months according to Correa, Vasco da Gama pursued his way to India.

The Portuguese ships arrived off Calicut in June or August, 1498. The powerful Hindu ruler on the Malabar coast, who was known as the Zamorin,[1] had his capital in that city. His body-guard and most of his aristocracy consisted of Nairs and Nestorian Christians, but all commerce was in the hands of the Muhammadan merchants. These Muhammadans were Moplas, or descendants of Arab traders who had long settled upon the Malabar coast. They quickly perceived that if Vasco da Gama could make his way direct from Portugal to India other Portuguese ships could do the same, and that then their lucrative monopoly of the Indian trade with Europe by way of the Red Sea or the Persian Gulf, would be at an end. They therefore intrigued with the Hindu ministers of the Zamorin to repulse the endeavours of Vasco da Gama to procure a cargo of Indian commodities for his ships, and it was only after much difficulty and some danger that he was able to take on board an inadequate amount of merchandise. On leaving Calicut the Portuguese Admiral visited Cannanore, and he eventually reached Melinda on his way home in January, 1499. He had a long and difficult passage back to Europe; in the island of Terceira his beloved brother Paulo da Gama died, and when he got safely to Lisbon at the end of August, 1499, he had with him but fifty-five of the companions who had started with him on his adventurous voyage.

King Emmanuel of Portugal, and his people, received Vasco da Gama with the utmost enthusiasm. The dreams of Prince Henry the Navigator and of King John II were fulfilled. King Emmanuel took the title of 'Lord of the Conquest, Navigation and Commerce of Ethiopia, Arabia, Persia and India,' which was confirmed to him by a Bull of Pope Alexander VI in 1502, and he commenced the erection of the superb church at Belem as a token of his gratitude to Heaven. On Vasco da Gama the King conferred well deserved honours. He was granted the use of the prefix of *Dom* or Lord, then but rarely conferred; he was permitted to quarter the Royal Arms with his own; he was given the office of Admiral of the Indian Seas; and in the following reign, when the importance of his voyage became more manifest, he was created Count of Vidigueira.

King Emmanuel determined to take immediate advantage of the trade route

[1] The title Zamorin is a version of the Malayālim word *Tāmātiri* or *Tāmūri,* which is a modification of the Sanskrit *Sāmundri* 'the Sea King.'

opened to him by Dom Vasco da Gama's voyage. On March 9, 1500, a fine fleet of thirteen ships was despatched under the command of Pedro Alvares Cabral, well laden with merchandise, to trade with India. On his way out this Portuguese fleet was driven far to the westward, and to Cabral belongs the honour of discovering Brazil, which was eventually to become far more valuable to Portugal than the Indian trade. On leaving Brazil, Cabral followed the course taken by Dom Vasco da Gama, and with the help of pilots from Melinda anchored safely in the port of Calicut. At that place he established a factory or agency for the sale of the merchandise he had brought with him and for the purchase of Indian commodities, and then sailed for Cochin.

But the Mopla merchants were still the declared enemies of the Portuguese. They raised a riot in the city of Calicut, and Ayres Correa, the Portuguese agent, was killed with several of his associates. It is worthy of remark that this murderous attack was entirely the work of the Arab Moplas. The Hindu Zamorin showed no disinclination to trade with the Europeans; the Malabar Muhammadans, that is the natives who had been converted to Islám, did not share in the outrage, and one of their principal merchants even interfered to save the lives of Correa's children and of some of the Portuguese clerks.

Cabral then loaded his ships at Cannanore and Cochin, where Hindu Rájás, inferior in power to the Zamorin, but not so much subject to Mopla influence, ruled, and after burning some of the Indian ships in the harbour of Calicut he returned to Lisbon in July, 1501. Cabral had not been so fortunate as Vasco da Gama, for he only brought back five out of the thirteen ships which he had taken with him. But, on the other hand, he did what Vasco da Gama had feared to do, and in spite of the fate of Ayres Correa and his associates, Cabral left a Portuguese factor with a considerable staff at Cochin to purchase goods for despatch to Portugal by the next fleet which should arrive.

On the return of Cabral from India, King Emmanuel resolved to send once more to the East the famous captain who had discovered the direct sea route to India. It was obvious to the king that large profits were to be made by the Eastern trade, but at this early period he had formed no distinct idea as to the policy he would pursue. On one point only he was resolved. It was quite certain that Portuguese agents would have to be left at the places of export if a prosperous trade was to be developed, and it was therefore necessary to give a severe lesson to the Zamorin of Calicut for the murder of the Portuguese factor at his capital. Adequate protection to Portuguese agents could only be given by maintaining a strong force in the Indian Seas. Vasco da Gama was therefore ordered to punish the Zamorin and to leave a squadron of ships for the defence of the Portuguese factors.

The establishment of commerce was at this time the chief aim of the Portuguese in the East, as it was in the succeeding century the chief aim of the Dutch and the English. But in the same way that the Dutch and English East India Companies were compelled to become military powers in order to defend their local agents, so King Emmanuel of Portugal was obliged to provide for the military defence of the first Portuguese factors. It was the fierce enmity of the Muhammadan merchants which caused the early European traders to take the attitude of invaders. The original Portuguese visitors had no more idea of establishing a Portuguese power in the East than the original English adventurers of the reign of Elizabeth foresaw that their successors would become the rulers of India. The position of a military and ruling power was forced on the Portuguese as it was afterwards on the Dutch and the English.

In February, 1502, Dom Vasco da Gama, Admiral of the Indian Seas, set sail from Lisbon with twenty ships, of which five were lateen-rigged caravels or lightly built warships which he was directed to leave behind him in the East. The Admiral followed his previous course, and after renewing his friendship with the Chief of Melinda he reached the Indian coast in safety. He found that the Portuguese factor at Cochin and his clerks had laid in a good store of Indian commodities, and that they had been kindly treated by the Rájá of that city in spite of the threats of the Moplas of Calicut. He then proceeded to repeat the lesson which Cabral had given to the Zamorin, and after destroying, under circumstances of atrocious cruelty, the crew of a large ship belonging to a wealthy and important Muhammadan owner, he bombarded the city of Calicut.

The Ráni of Quilon, an important pepper port, sent a message requesting that the Portuguese would come to her port also to obtain goods. But Dom Vasco da Gama feared to offend the Rájá of Cochin by trading elsewhere, and it was only after receiving the express consent of the latter monarch that he took two shiploads of pepper from Quilon. Having taken on board a lucrative cargo Dom Vasco da Gama returned once more to Portugal, leaving behind him the squadron designed for that purpose under the command of one of his relations, Vicente Sodré.

The Admiral also made a treaty with the Rájá of Cannanore, a ruler nearly as powerful as the Rájá of Cochin, which provided that the former should never make war on the Rájá of Cochin, and should refuse to assist the Zamorin in case that powerful ruler undertook such an attack, and he also established a factory at Cannanore. Vicente Sodré cruised for some time on the Malabar coast, as he had been directed to do, and then sailed for the coast of Arabia in order to intercept the ships of Muhammadan merchants trading between India and Egypt. He had, however, but small success; for in the summer of 1503 his squadron was wrecked on the Abd-el-Khuri rocks off Socotra, three of his ships were lost, and Sodré himself was drowned.

In 1503 three separate squadrons were despatched to the East from Portugal under the command respectively of Affonso de Albuquerque, the future Governor, Francisco de Albuquerque, his cousin, and Antonio de Saldanha, the last of whom was ordered to explore the African coast and gave his name to Saldanha Bay. Francisco de Albuquerque, who arrived first in India, was only just in time to succour the Rájá of Cochin. The Zamorin of Calicut, as Vasco da Gama had foreseen, had attacked the Rájá of Cochin in force, at the instigation of the Moplas, as soon as Sodré's squadron had left the Malabar coast. The situation of the Cochin Rájá was one of peril. He had been driven from his capital and was being besieged in the island of Vypín, and he welcomed the arrival of the ships of Francisco de Albuquerque with cries of joy.

The Portuguese met with little difficulty in defeating the army of the Zamorin and in restoring their ally, the Rájá of Cochin, to his dominions. But the extremity of the danger had been such that the two Albuquerques built a strong fort of wood and mud, mounted with artillery, at Cochin; and when they departed they left behind them not only a squadron of war-ships, as Vasco da Gama had done in the previous year, but also a garrison of trained soldiers for the new fort, both under the command of Duarte Pacheco. The two cousins Albuquerque had more than one difference of opinion, and Affonso, after sailing to Quilon, where he made a treaty with the Ráni and established a factory, returned to Portugal with his squadron, without waiting for Francisco.

No more valiant warrior illustrated the glory of the Portuguese name than Pacheco. The Zamorin of Calicut, as soon as the Albuquerques had left the coast, advanced against Cochin with a more powerful army than he had set on foot in the previous year. Pacheco had only 150 Portuguese soldiers, but nevertheless he inspired perfect confidence into the mind of his ally, the Cochin Rájá. That king, at the request of the Portuguese commander, abandoned his first idea of deserting his capital, and placed all his resources at the disposition of Pacheco, who repulsed every assault which the Zamorin made upon Cochin, and defeated his troops in four pitched battles beneath the walls of the city. The valour of the Portuguese greatly impressed the Zamorin, who witnessed the last of these battles, and the Hindu ruler soon repented his compliance with the demands of the Mopla merchants.

After defeating the Calicut troops on land Pacheco took the personal command of his squadron at sea, and defeated the Calicut fleet of fifty-two ships. The news of these battles spread abroad through India. Many Rájás in the interior sent envoys to the Portuguese commander, and the Zamorin himself earnestly sued for peace. The prestige of the Portuguese was assured by Pacheco's victories, and from this time forth for nearly a century the inhabitants of Southern India recognised that the Portuguese were stronger than themselves, and were eager to trade with them or to make alliances.

Pacheco increased his reputation by a daring march to Quilon, where he rescued the Portuguese factor from much danger; for at Quilon, as at all the ports along the coast, the Moplas showed an unrelenting hatred to the European agents. When Lopo Soares de Albergaria, son of the Chancellor of Portugal, who commanded the squadron sent from Portugal in 1504, reached the Malabar coast he found the Indian ports ringing with news of Pacheco's victories. He once more bombarded Calicut, and then returned to Portugal, bringing with him a rich cargo and also the gallant Portuguese commander. It is a lasting disgrace to King Emmanuel that he neglected to reward the hero of Cochin according to his merits. He gave his faithful servant a distinguished reception, and had sermons preached in his honour in every church of Portugal, but eventually, like Camoens and other famous Portuguese warriors, Pacheco was left to die in poverty and misery.

It was after the return of Pacheco, and probably owing to that brave man's advice, that King Emmanuel in 1505 inaugurated a new departure in the relations between Portugal and the East. Pacheco's victories made it evident that it was not only possible for Portuguese garrisons and local squadrons to defend the Portuguese factors, but that they could defeat and conquer powerful native monarchs. A conception of the ease by which a Portuguese empire could be established in the East was now grasped by King Emmanuel. His ideas were still mainly commercial, but he began to perceive also that the safe maintenance of trade and commerce would necessarily involve a regular war to the death with the Muhammadan powers who had reaped the greatest profit from the trade of the East with Europe. Hitherto the Portuguese in India had striven with the Muhammadan Moplas settled on the Malabar coast; but it now became apparent that the Muhammadans of Egypt, Persia, and Arabia would come to the help of their co-religionists. Emmanuel decided therefore to maintain a more powerful army and navy in Asia than he had yet despatched to the Eastern seas, and to replace annual expeditions by a local establishment.

Such a force had to be commanded by an experienced general, who should also be a man of rank, in order to exercise undisputed sway over the whole resources of Portugal in the East. For this important office the king first selected Tristão da Cunha, a daring and skilful commander and navigator. But Tristão da Cunha was struck with temporary blindness, and King Emmanuel then chose Dom Francisco de Almeida, a member of one of the most illustrious families of Portugal. Almeida when he sailed received only the title of Chief Captain, but on his arrival at Cannanore on September 12, 1505, he took the high-sounding title of Viceroy of Cochin, Cannanore, and Quilon.

The great Portuguese nobleman looked upon the situation of affairs in a different light to his predecessors. He was not satisfied with the idea of protecting the Portuguese trade which had been established, but considered it his duty to destroy the Muhammadan traders and to secure for his countrymen the entire command of the Eastern seas. Since it was necessary for the Portuguese fleets to have some safe ports at which they could refit before and after crossing the Indian Ocean, he built a strong fortress at Quiloa (Kilwa), about 200 miles south of Zanzibar, and made the Chief of Mombassa between Zanzibar and Melinda tributary. He also organised, for the first time, a regular Portuguese Indian pilot service, for he felt it to be a weakness to the Portuguese to be dependent on native pilots like the men who had shown Vasco da Gama the way across the Indian Ocean.

Having firmly established the Portuguese power on the African coast, Dom Francisco de Almeida continued on his way to India. His fleet consisted of fourteen ships and six caravels, and carried 1500 soldiers. On reaching the Malabar coast he first punished the Rájás of Honáwar and Cannanore, and then established his seat of government at Cochin. The Viceroy next sent his son Dom Lourenço de Almeida, who had been appointed Chief Captain of the Indian Sea, to attack Quilon. The Moplas in that city, in spite of the lesson taught to them by Pacheco, had not ceased their intrigues against the Portuguese; and soon after Almeida's arrival they rose in insurrection and killed Antonio de Sá, the factor, and twelve other Portuguese subjects. Dom Lourenço, who was but eighteen years of age, and who soon made for himself a reputation for daring and valour unequalled in the East, bombarded and practically destroyed the city of Quilon. The young captain then visited the island of Ceylon, which had not yet been explored by the Europeans. The native prince on whose coasts he landed received Lourenço with great pomp, recognised the suzerainty of the King of Portugal and promised to provide the Portuguese ships with cargoes of cinnamon. From Ceylon also Dom Lourenço brought the first elephant ever sent to Portugal.

After his return to Cochin the Viceroy despatched his gallant son to meet a fresh fleet which had been prepared by the Zamorin of Calicut. On March 18, 1506, with but eleven ships of war under his command, Lourenço de Almeida attacked the Zamorin's fleet of eighty-four ships and a hundred and twenty prahs or galleys. The sea-fight which followed was chiefly an artillery combat; most of the Zamorin's ships were sunk, and it is said that 3000 Muhammadans perished and not more than six or eight Portuguese. The young captain sailed northward with his victorious fleet, but was repulsed in an attack on Dábhol, an important port belonging to the Muhammadan King of Bijápur. In the following year Dom Lourenço de Almeida continued his series of victories, and on November 23, 1507, with the assistance of Tristão da Cunha, who had just arrived in India, he sacked the port of Ponáni, then, as it still is, a religious centre of the Mopla community.

Meanwhile the danger which King Emmanuel had foreseen was coming to pass. The Mameluke Sultan of Egypt perceived that his income from the passage of the Indian trade through Cairo was seriously diminishing, and he resolved to make a great effort to expel the daring European intruders from the Eastern seas. He therefore prepared a large fleet, which was placed under the command of the Emir Husain, an admiral of high reputation, whom the Portuguese chroniclers call Mir Hocem. This was the first regular war fleet which the Portuguese had yet met. The fleets of the Zamorin, which Pacheco and Dom Lourenço de Almeida had defeated, consisted only of merchant ships roughly adapted for war by the Mopla traders of Calicut. The fleet of the Emir Husain, on the other hand, was a regular war fleet; it was largely manned by sailors who had experience in fighting with Christian fleets in the Mediterranean, and who understood the use of artillery quite as well as the Portuguese.

The Egyptian admiral in 1508 sailed from the Red Sea for the coast of Gujarát, where the Muhammadan King of Ahmadábád and the Muhammadan Nawáb of Diu, Málik Ayaz, had promised to receive and assist him. Dom Lourenço de Almeida was unable to prevent the junction of the Egyptian and the Diu fleets, and on their approach to his station in the port of Chaul he boldly sailed out and attacked them. His numbers were totally inadequate, but he had received express orders from his father to endeavour to prevent the allies from coming south to Calicut to join the Zamorin. For two days the Portuguese maintained a running fight, but Dom Lourenço de Almeida soon found that he had to deal with more experienced and warlike foes than the merchant captains he had so often defeated. His ship was surrounded on every side; his leg was broken by a cannon-ball at the commencement of the action; nevertheless he had himself placed upon a chair at the foot of the mainmast and gave his orders as coolly as ever. Shortly afterwards a second cannon-ball struck him in the breast, and the young hero, who was not yet twenty-one, expired, in the words of Camoens, without knowing what the word surrender meant. Málik Ayaz treated the Portuguese prisoners whom he took kindly. He wrote to the Viceroy regretting that he was unable to find Dom Lourenço's body to give it honourable burial, and congratulated the father on the glory the son had acquired in his last combat.

At this juncture Affonso de Albuquerque, who had been sent from Lisbon with a commission to succeed Dom Francisco de Almeida, at the close of the latter's three years tenure of office, made his claims known. The Viceroy, however, refused to surrender his office or to abandon the government until he had avenged his son's death. Albuquerque told the Viceroy that it was his privilege to fight the Egyptian fleet, but he felt for the father's feelings and allowed Francisco de Almeida to sail northwards without further pressing his rights. The Viceroy first relieved the fortress of Cannanore, which was being besieged by the Moplas and gallantly defended by Lourenço de Brito, and he then attacked Dábhol with a fleet of nineteen ships. He stormed Dábhol and wreaked a horrible vengeance, which passed into a proverb, on the inhabitants in December, 1508. On February 2, 1509, Dom Francisco de Almeida came up with the united fleet of the Muhammadans under Emir Husain and Málik Ayaz off Diu, and after a battle which lasted the whole day a great victory was won, in which the Muhammadans are said to have lost 3000 men and the Portuguese only twenty-two.

After the victory the powerful Muhammadan King of Ahmadábád or Gujarát, Mahmúd Sháh Begára, disavowed the conduct of Málik Ayaz, his tributary, and made peace with the Portuguese. He refused to surrender the Emir, but he gave up the Portuguese prisoners who had been taken in the previous engagement as well as the remains of the Egyptian fleet. On his return to Cochin, Dom Francisco de Almeida again refused to hand over the government to Albuquerque, and imprisoned his destined successor in the fortress of Cannanore.

However, on the arrival of Dom Fernão de Coutinho, Marshal of Portugal, the Viceroy was forced to abandon this attitude, and he left Cochin on November 10, 1509. On his way home he was obliged to put in to refit at Saldanha Bay, where his sailors had a dispute with some Kaffirs whose sheep they had stolen. Dom Francisco de Almeida went to their help, but he was struck down and killed with an assegai. Thus died the first Viceroy of Portuguese India on March 1, 1510, and it is a strange irony of fate that the famous conqueror of the Muhammadan fleet, who by his victory assured the power of the Portuguese in the East, should die by the hands of ignorant African savages.

The policy of the first Viceroy of India was not so grandiose as that of his successor. He did not believe in building many forts or attempting to establish direct government in the East. He argued that Portugal had not sufficient inhabitants to occupy many posts, and his view was that the Portuguese fleets should hold the sea and thus protect the factories on land. Any idea of establishing a Portuguese dominion in Asia seemed visionary to the first Portuguese Viceroy, and in this respect his policy differed entirely from that of his successor, Affonso de Albuquerque.

A letter from Francisco de Almeida to Emmanuel is published by Senhor Lopes de Mendonça in the *Annaes das Sciencias e Letteras* for April, 1858, and reveals the Viceroy's policy. In it he says:—

> 'With respect to the fortress in Quilon, the greater the number of fortresses you hold, the weaker will be your power; let all our forces be on the sea; because if we should not be powerful at sea (which may the Lord forbid) everything will at once be against us; and if the King of Cochin should desire to be disloyal, he would be at once destroyed, because our past wars were waged with animals; now we have wars with the Venetians and the Turks of the Sultan. And as regards the King of Cochin, I have already written to your Highness that it would be well to have a strong castle in Cranganore on a passage of the river which goes to Calicut, because it would hinder the transport by that way of a single peck of pepper. With the force we have at sea we will discover what these new enemies may be, for I trust in the mercy of God that He will remember us, since all the rest is of little importance. Let it be known for certain that as long as you may be powerful at sea, you will hold India as yours; and if you do not possess this power, little will avail you a fortress on shore; and as to expelling the Moors (Muhammadans) from the country, I have found the right way to do it, but it is a long story, and it will be done when the Lord pleases and will thus be served.'

CHAPTER II

THE EARLY CAREER OF ALBUQUERQUE

The name of Albuquerque was already famous in the history of Castile and of Portugal before the birth of the great man who increased its lustre. It is not without interest to examine the history of the family, for it illustrates in a remarkable manner the origin of the most noble houses of the Peninsula. It is besides always of interest to study the ancestry of a great man, for the qualities which distinguished him are generally to be perceived also in former members of his family.

The family of Albuquerque derived its origin from Dom Affonso Sanches, an illegitimate son of King Diniz or Denis, *The Labourer,* and a beautiful Gallician lady, Dona Aldonsa de Sousa. King Denis is one of the most remarkable figures in the early history of Portugal. He ascended the throne in 1279, just after the Moors had been thoroughly conquered and Portugal had attained its European limits by the annexation of the Algarves. He reigned for nearly half a century, and, as his *sobriquet* indicates, was a man of peace. He devoted himself to improving the internal administration of the country, to bringing waste lands under cultivation and to encouraging commerce. But he had another side to his character. King Denis was one of the earliest of the Portuguese poets. He wrote in the style of the Troubadours, and imitated their morality as well as their verse. The mother of Dom Affonso Sanches was one of the most famous of the king's mistresses, and was very dearly beloved by him. He showered favours on his illegitimate children, and made Affonso Sanches Mordomo-Mor, or Lord High Steward, of his realm, to the extreme wrath of his legitimate heir, who was afterwards King Affonso IV.

The latter years of the reign of King Denis were embittered by war between the king and the heir apparent. As soon as the latter ascended the throne in 1325 he banished his half-brothers from Portugal and confiscated all the lands which his father had granted to them. Dom Affonso Sanches, who was a renowned warrior, took refuge at the court of the King of Castile, and there married Dona Theresa Martins, daughter of João Affonso Telles de Menezes and granddaughter of Sancho III, King of Castile. With her he obtained, in addition to other lands, the Castle of Albuquerque, near Badajoz, which he entirely rebuilt. His son João Affonso took the name of Albuquerque from this castle; he married Dona Isabel de Menezes and became Mordomo-Mor to King Pedro *the Cruel,* of Castile and Leon.

The legitimate issue of this great lord, who was one of the most important figures in the history of the time, founded the famous Spanish house of Albuquerque, which gave many distinguished generals and statesmen to the service of the State. He had also certain illegitimate children, who returned to Portugal. The two daughters of this illegitimate family, Dona Beatrice and Dona Maria, were ladies whose beauty was famous, and they married two brothers of Leonor, the queen of King Ferdinand of Portugal, the Counts of Barcellos and Neiva. Their brother, Fernão Affonso de Albuquerque, became Grand Master of the Portuguese Knights of the Order of Santiago. The illegitimate daughter of the Grand Master, Dona Theresa, married Vasco Martins da Cunha, who, by his first marriage, was great-grandfather of the famous navigator, Tristão da Cunha; his granddaughter married Gonçalo Vaz de Mello, and his great-granddaughter, Dona Leonor, João Gonçalvez de Gomide. The husband of the last-mentioned lady took her famous surname of Albuquerque, and was the father by her of a numerous family, one of whom, Pedro de Albuquerque, became Lord High Admiral of Portugal. His eldest son, Gonçalo de Albuquerque, succeeded his father as Lord of Villa Verde, and married Dona Leonor de Menezes, daughter of Dom Alvaro Gonçalvez de Athaide.

Affonso de Albuquerque, who, it may be remarked, always spelt his name Alboquerque, which is the version adopted by the early Portuguese writers, was the second son of this marriage. This sketch of the history of his ancestors shows to what great families the future governor of Portuguese Asia was allied; the frequent tale of unlawful love to be observed throughout it is a feature common to the records of the most illustrious captains of his time. His elder brother, Fernão de Albuquerque, married a daughter of Diogo da Silva, and had two daughters, one of whom married Dom Martinho de Noronha, and the other Jorge Barreto, both names which often occur in the history of the Portuguese in the East. His next brother, Alvaro, took Holy Orders and became Prior of Villa Verde, and his youngest brother, Martim, was killed by his side at Arzila. His elder sister, Constance, married Dom Fernão de Noronha, and his younger sister, Isabel, married Pedro da Silva Relle.

Affonso de Albuquerque was born at Alhandra, a beautiful village about eighteen miles from Lisbon, in 1453. He was brought up at the court of King Affonso V, where he is said to have been a page. He was certainly educated with the king's sons, and became in his early years a friend of Prince John, afterwards John II. He was not only a thorough master of his own language, which, as his despatches show, he wrote with force and elegance, but he also studied Latin and Mathematics. The latter science was an especial favourite of his and very useful to him during his voyages, in assisting him to master the technicalities of navigation, so that he could, in time of need, act as a pilot. The court of Affonso V was well calculated to stir the knightly spirit of a lad. The king himself was known as *El Rey Cavalleiro* or the *Chivalrous King;* his one delight was in war, and he was never tired of reading the romances of mediaeval chivalry and trying to follow the example of its heroes. King Affonso V had also a great taste for literature: he founded the famous library at Evora, and his answer to the chronicler, Acenheiro, who asked how he should write the chronicle of his reign, illustrated his disposition; for he answered simply, 'Tell the truth.'

In 1471 Affonso de Albuquerque, then a young man of eighteen, served in

King Affonso's third expedition to Morocco, in which the Portuguese took the cities of Tangier, Anafe, and Arzila. In the last of these towns he remained for some years as an officer of the garrison. This was an excellent school for the training of an officer, and Albuquerque there learnt not only his military duties but his hatred for the Muhammadans. It was in the garrisons in Morocco that the Portuguese soldiers and captains, who were to prove their valour in the East, served their apprenticeship to war; and the ten years which Albuquerque spent there were not years thrown away.

In 1481, when his friend John II succeeded to the throne, Affonso de Albuquerque returned to Portugal, and was appointed to the high court office of Estribeiro-Mor, which is equivalent to the post of Master of the Horse or Chief Equerry. This office he held throughout the reign of John II, and his close intimacy with that wise and great king ripened his intellect and trained him to thoughts of great enterprises. John II was always thinking of the direct sea route to India; Albuquerque shared his hopes, and there can be no doubt that the grand schemes for establishing Portuguese influence in Asia which he afterwards conceived, had their origin in his intimacy with *The Perfect King*. He served on the fleet sent to the Gulf of Taranto to defend King Ferdinand of Naples against an invasion of the Turks; and in 1489 he commanded the defence of the fortress of Graciosa, on the coast of Morocco, against an attack of the Moors.

On the death of John II, in 1495, Affonso de Albuquerque, like the other intimates of the deceased sovereign, was looked upon coldly by King Emmanuel. This cannot be wondered at, for John II had murdered Emmanuel's elder brother with his own hand, and had even thought of ousting Emmanuel himself from the throne by legitimatising his natural son Dom Jorge. In 1495, Affonso de Albuquerque returned to Arzila and served there for some time longer against the Moors. At this period his younger brother Martim was killed by his side in a foray, and the boy's death further increased Albuquerque's personal hatred for all Muhammadans. After this catastrophe Affonso went back to Portugal, and since King Emmanuel was now firmly fixed upon the throne, he did not further hesitate to use the services of so experienced an officer.

In 1503 Affonso de Albuquerque was for the first time despatched to the Indian seas, in which he was at a later date to perform his great feats of arms. In this year he only commanded, as has been said, a little squadron of three ships, and played a part inferior to that played by his cousin Francisco de Albuquerque, the son of John II's Lord High Admiral. His chief act of importance at that time was his commencing to build a fort at Cochin to defend the local Portuguese factory; but he also visited Quilon and appointed a factor in that city. Nevertheless, though he did not do much in 1503, he learnt much that was useful to him in subsequent years. He saw for the first time the Indian coast, and was enabled to study on the spot the problems presented by the establishment of the Portuguese.

He also experienced the difficulties of a divided command. He quarrelled seriously with his cousin, and eventually, in spite of the king's direct orders to the contrary, he left the Malabar coast without waiting for his colleague. On leaving Cochin he took the bold step of shaping his course for Mozambique. Hitherto the

Portuguese fleets had always struck the African coast higher up in order to make the passage across the Indian Ocean as short as possible. Nevertheless, guided by a Muhammadan pilot, Albuquerque reached Mozambique in safety, and after a perilous voyage along the West Coast of Africa, arrived at Lisbon in July, 1504. His cousin, who had delayed his departure, was lost at sea with his squadron without anyone ever knowing where or how they perished.

On his return to Portugal Affonso de Albuquerque was very favourably received by King Emmanuel. He encouraged the king's idea of securing the monopoly of the Indian trade, and insisted that the only way by which this could be done was to close the previous routes by the Red Sea and the Persian Gulf. Modern ideas of commercial freedom were unknown even in the last century, when the River Scheldt was closed by treaties assented to by the chief European powers; and it was hardly to be expected that in the sixteenth century the general good of humanity should be preferred to national considerations. King Emmanuel therefore entered into Albuquerque's schemes for destroying the commerce carried on by the Muhammadans with India, and resolved to despatch the chief author of this policy to the East.

Accordingly, in 1506, when Tristão da Cunha was ordered to the East with a fleet of eleven ships, Albuquerque accompanied him with a separate squadron of five ships destined to operate on the coasts of Arabia. Albuquerque was placed under the command of Da Cunha until the island of Socotra should be conquered and garrisoned by the Portuguese, after which event Da Cunha was to proceed to India to load his ships. Albuquerque was then to assume an independent command, and after doing what he could to close the Red Sea to commerce was to go to India and take over the supreme command from the Viceroy, Dom Francisco de Almeida. These secret orders were not communicated to the Viceroy immediately, and Albuquerque was directed not to present his commission until Almeida had completed three years of government. At the same time a powerful fleet was despatched to the Mediterranean, under the Prior of Crato, who was instructed to attack the Turks, and thus to prevent them from sending sailors to assist the Muhammadans in the Eastern seas. Selim I, who was then ruling at Constantinople, was at issue with the Mameluke Sultan of Egypt, whom a few years later he conquered, but the opposition between them was not understood in Portugal, and it was believed that the Turks would be inclined to assist the Egyptians.

On April 5, 1506, Tristão da Cunha and Affonso de Albuquerque set sail from the Tagus. Differences between the two commanders soon appeared. Albuquerque's own pilot had fled to Castile, after murdering his wife, and, since Tristão da Cunha refused to give him another pilot, the future Governor of Portuguese India had to navigate his own vessel. But the difference between them was not due alone to this personal dispute—the two men were of essentially different temperaments. Tristão da Cunha was before all things an explorer; his hope was to discover fresh countries for his royal master. Albuquerque was, on the other hand, a statesman, fully impressed with the importance of the mission on which he was sent and determined to subordinate everything else to it. This radical difference soon made itself felt. When the united fleet reached Mozambique, news was brought to the principal commander by Ruy Pereira Coutinho that he had discovered an island which seemed rich in cloves and other spices. This island he had named the Island of San Lourenço, and it is the island now known as Madagascar. Tristão da Cunha, in spite of the remonstrances of Albuquerque, who refused to accompany him, went off at once to explore the new land. But, after a perilous voyage, he abandoned his purpose and joined Albuquerque to carry out the first aim of the expedition, the conquest of the island of Socotra.

As they made their way north along the African coast, they paid a visit to Melinda and renewed the treaty of friendship between the Chief of that place and the Portuguese. The Chief of Melinda told the Portuguese captains that the Chiefs of Mombassa and Angoja caused him much annoyance for his friendship with the Portuguese, and begged that they would take vengeance on them. In accordance with this request, the Portuguese sacked and burnt the city of Angoja, the Chief of which place was 'a Moorish merchant who came from abroad, but as he was very rich he had made himself lord of all that land.'[2] The fleet then proceeded to Braboa, or Brava, where the Muhammadan ruler refused to acknowledge the supremacy of or pay tribute to the King of Portugal. The place was therefore attacked and burnt by the Portuguese sailors. In this engagement Tristão da Cunha was wounded, and at his own request was knighted by Affonso de Albuquerque on the spot where he had received his wound.

After these acts of summary vengeance the Portuguese fleet proceeded to Socotra. This island, which is situated off Cape Guardafui, in such a position as to command the Gulf of Aden, had been discovered by Diogo Fernandes Pereira two years before, and had been visited by Antonio de Saldanha. They had reported the existence of Christians on the island, who wished to place themselves under the authority of the King of Portugal. King Emmanuel had for this reason, as well as on account of its importance in commanding the Gulf of Aden, ordered that a fortress should be built upon the island, and had given a commission as Governor to Albuquerque's nephew, Dom Affonso de Noronha. The Portuguese found a strong castle on the island, defended by a Muhammadan garrison of 150 men. It was stormed, after an engagement lasting seven hours, in which Albuquerque himself was wounded. A well-armed fortress, to which the name of St. Michael was given, was then erected, as well as a Franciscan monastery, and the somewhat degraded Christians, who are described by Marco Polo as belonging to the Greek Church, were in great numbers baptized in the Catholic religion. On August 1, 1507, Tristão da Cunha, having completed the first task appointed to him, sailed away to India to take in cargo, leaving behind him Affonso de Albuquerque with six ships. On his way back to Portugal the great explorer, who did not again go to the East, discovered the solitary island in the Atlantic which bears his name. He was received with great honour, and was sent as Portuguese Ambassador to Pope Leo X. His fame was such that the Pope begged him to take command of an expedition against the Turks. But the explorer felt he was not a great soldier, and declined the flattering offer. He eventually returned to Portugal, and died a member of the King's Privy Council in 1540.

[2] Albuquerque's *Commentaries,* vol. i. p. 36.

On the departure of Da Cunha, Albuquerque provided for the government of the island of Socotra. He divided the palm-groves which had belonged to the Muhammadans among the native Christians, and those which had belonged to the mosque he gave to the Christian churches. He then refitted his ships and left Socotra, with the intention of intercepting the Muhammadan merchant-vessels on their way from India to Egypt. Before long he began to have disputes with the captains of his principal ships. His own flagship, the *Cirne,* was in good control, and he was always bravely helped in his difficulties by his gallant young nephew, Dom Antonio de Noronha. But the captains of the other ships which had accompanied him from Portugal—Francisco de Tavora, Antonio do Campo, Affonso Lopes da Costa, and Manoel Telles—were inclined to resent his authority, and objected to cruising on the barren coast of Arabia instead of fetching lucrative cargoes from India. Their opposition was fomented by a famous captain, João da Nova, the discoverer of the island of St. Helena, who had come to the East with Dom Francisco de Almeida, and who showed himself throughout his career in Asia to be Albuquerque's most implacable enemy. He had joined the fleet at Socotra, in command of one of the finest Portuguese ships ever launched, the *Flor de la Mar,* and had been directed, much to his chagrin, by Tristão da Cunha to remain with Albuquerque.

Being in need of supplies, the Portuguese commander next resolved to shape his course for the Persian Gulf. He had at first intended to penetrate the Red Sea, but having become possessed of a chart of the Persian Gulf made by a Muhammadan pilot, he bent his way thither instead. The important city of Ormuz, at the mouth of the Persian Gulf, was at this time one of the great centres of the Eastern trade. Not only did a certain portion of trade for Europe pass through it, but the large and important commerce carried on between Persia and India was concentrated there. The wealth and prosperity of Ormuz is described in glowing terms by all early travellers in Asia, and it is called in ancient books 'the richest jewel set in the ring of the world.' Albuquerque quickly grasped the importance of getting possession of Ormuz; he saw that he might by that means not only intercept the Indian trade which went that way, but might also establish a direct trade between Persia and Europe. Persian commodities, as well as those of India, were much valued in Europe. Hitherto they had generally passed through the hands of the merchants of the Levant; but the Portuguese statesman at once perceived that it would be possible to convey them more cheaply by the direct sea-route to Portugal.

The first place at which Albuquerque touched on his way to Ormuz was Calayate (Kālhāt), which the inhabitants described as the door of Ormuz. It was a great resort for shipping, and exported horses and dates in large quantities to India. Albuquerque was favourably received there, and took in supplies. Following the coast, the Portuguese bombarded Curiate and Muscat, where they were badly received, and with atrocious cruelty Albuquerque ordered the ears and noses of the Muhammadan prisoners to be cut off before they were released. On October 10, 1507, he reached Ormuz, and there entered into negotiations with Cogeatar (Khojah Atár), the Prime Minister of the King of Ormuz. The Portuguese commander first demanded that the native ruler should declare himself a vassal of the King of Portugal and should promise to pay tribute to him. In this he was successful. He then demanded a site on which to erect a fortress to be garrisoned by a Portuguese force. The foundations of this fortress were marked out on October 24, 1507, and the building was undertaken by native labour under Portuguese superintendence. Meanwhile, the disgust of the Portuguese captains increased; they protested against the conduct of Albuquerque, and spoke openly of leaving him and going by themselves to India. In consequence of this conduct Albuquerque suspended Francisco de Tavora from the command of his ship. Nor were the sailors less mutinous: four of them escaped to the native minister and informed Cogeatar of the dissensions which prevailed. Albuquerque haughtily demanded the immediate surrender of the deserters, and threatened to attack Ormuz in case of a refusal.

On the news of the contemplated assault the rebellious captains, on January 5, 1508, presented a remonstrance to their commander, which is so characteristic of the difficulties which beset Albuquerque on every side, and so illustrative of the impression formed by his character, that it is worth quoting in full:—

> 'Sir,—We do this in writing, because by word of mouth we dare not, as you always answer us so passionately; and for all that you, Sir, have frequently told us that the King gives you no orders to take counsel with us, yet this business is of so great an importance, that we consider ourselves obliged to offer you our advice; did we not do so, we should be worthy of punishment. Now, because this war, in which you are now desirous of engaging, is very much opposed to the interest of the King, our Lord, we consider that your Excellency ought to weigh well, before entering upon it, how little Cogeatar is to blame for objecting to have against all reason to pay down in ready money 15,000 cruzados of revenue every year, contrary to the honour of such a large city and kingdom; yet, if notwithstanding all this, your Excellency is determined to prosecute the war, and break the peace and agreement which has been made with him, it is our opinion that you ought not to do so; for it would be more to the service of the King, our Lord, if we were now to quit this city and temporize with Cogeatar, and in the course of the year return in strength in order to subdue it, and confirm our hold upon it, than to destroy it for ever. And if, in spite of all we can say, your Excellency is bent upon entering into this war, see you that it be with all the circumspection and assurance that the fleet can command, in that it is more conducive to the interest of our said Lord to obtain possession and not to destroy the city now, since it can be destroyed at any time we please; because, in case of your Excellency's landing in Ormuz or at the city we are determined not to go with you, nor enter into such a war, nor such designs, and that this may be known for certain, and we be not able to deny it hereafter, we all sign our names here: this day, the 5th of the month of January, 1508.

João da Nova,
Antonio do Campo,
Affonso Lopes da Costa,
Francisco de Tavora,
Manoel Telles.'[3]

It need hardly be said that Albuquerque refused to listen to this remonstrance. Francisco de Tavora, whom he had pardoned and restored to his command, declared himself on Albuquerque's side, and in a few hours all the captains

> 'begged him very earnestly to do them the favour to forget it all, for their passion had blinded them, and all were ready to serve him in the war and to perform all that he might require of them.'[4]

Albuquerque accordingly attacked Ormuz and defeated the troops who had assembled to prevent his landing; but Cogeatar knew of the discontent of the captains, and steadfastly refused to surrender the deserters. With João da Nova the situation soon became still more strained. This captain was undoubtedly the leader of the malcontents, and at last, after a disgraceful scene, Albuquerque ordered him under arrest. An enquiry was made into his conduct and that of his ship's crew, and in the words of the *Commentaries,*

> 'the captain and all the men were found to be so guilty that it was thought to be better counsel to forgive them, considering the times they had fallen upon, and the necessity there was of them, than to punish them as they deserved; ... and he [Albuquerque] ordered them to return to the ship, and released João da Nova from custody and returned him his captaincy, not caring to hear any more of his guilt, but leaving the punishment of it for the King to settle, although he had, in the instructions given to him, granted him power for all.'[5]

These troubles in his fleet caused Albuquerque to abandon his project of building a castle at Ormuz, and he therefore sailed away, in April 1508, to intercept the Muhammadan merchant-ships on their way from India. The disputes with his captains still continued, and three of them—Antonio do Campo, Affonso Lopes da Costa, and Manoel Telles—deserted him and went to India. Their desertion was soon followed by that of João da Nova, whose departure deprived him of the finest ship in his squadron. With his diminished force of only two ships Albuquerque sailed to Socotra, where he found the garrison suffering from want of provisions, having nothing to eat but palm-leaves and wild fruit. He then cruised for some time in the Gulf of Aden, and eventually he finally disgraced Francisco de Tavora, his sole remaining captain, who disgusted him by further mutinous behaviour.

After cruising for four months in the Gulf of Aden, during which time he only took one prize, he proceeded once more to Calayate (Kālhāt). The governor of the place was an intimate friend of Cogeatar, and did not receive the Portuguese as

[3] Albuquerque's *Commentaries,* vol. i. pp. 169, 170.
[4] Albuquerque's *Commentaries,* vol. i. p. 172.
[5] Albuquerque's *Commentaries,* vol. i. p. 189.

favourably as he had done in the previous year. On observing symptoms of resistance Albuquerque promptly attacked the city, and after a furious engagement, in which Dom Antonio da Noronha especially distinguished himself, Calayate was sacked and burnt. The ships in the harbour were also destroyed, and with great barbarity the ears and noses of all the Muhammadans who were taken prisoners were cut off.

Albuquerque then went on to Ormuz, where he heard the news of the sea-fight off Chaul, in which Dom Lourenço de Almeida had been killed. Cogeatar also forwarded to Albuquerque a letter which he had received from Dom Francisco de Almeida, the Portuguese Viceroy. In this letter Albuquerque's conduct in the previous year was greatly blamed, and the Viceroy declared his intention of chastising Albuquerque, 'in order that he may learn that wheresoever he shall receive honour, and give a writing on the King's behalf, he ought not to alter it, for the King of Portugal is not a liar, and it is necessary that his captain should not depart from his commands.'[6] In enclosing this letter to Albuquerque, Cogeatar announced his intention of informing the Viceroy that Albuquerque was a traitor to the King of Portugal. In reply to these communications, Albuquerque sent a haughty letter, in which he defended his conduct during the previous year:—

> 'Have I not already many a time told thee,' he wrote, 'that I was no corsair but Captain-General of the King of Portugal, an old man and a peaceable one?... In what is stated in the Persian letter [from the Viceroy] about my not daring to go to him, but that I went instead to Socotra, know of a certainty that I have fear of no one except of my King; but, on the contrary, I tell thee that the captain who knew both how to obtain this kingdom, and conquer a king in battle, and make him tributary to the King of Portugal, will be treated with great honour let him go whithersoever he will, and the Viceroy knows that I have performed my duty in proceeding to succour the fortress of Socotra, as my King had ordered me, and that I had not now fled, had I not gone to seek for the supplies which the captains carried away from me when they departed, leaving thy fleet of seventy sail against me, although I commanded them to make for it and destroy it; but this they would not do, and well it was that it turned out so, since between thee and them there was such amity.'[7]

Albuquerque then promised to demand a strict account some day from Cogeatar for his behaviour; he swore not to cut his beard until he had completed the fortress at Ormuz, and, after capturing a rich merchant-ship, he sailed for India. He had spent two years and eight months at sea, and was now to show his capacity in a wider sphere.

While Albuquerque was establishing the power of Portugal on the coasts of Arabia and in the Persian Gulf, Almeida was being prejudiced against him. The deserter and rebel captains met with a favourable reception from the Viceroy.

[6] Albuquerque's *Commentaries,* vol. i. p. 227.

[7] Albuquerque's *Commentaries,* vol. i. pp. 237, 238.

They described Albuquerque to him 'as a very harsh sort of a man, and very hasty, without bearing in mind the honour of his men,'[8] and declared that he had exceeded his orders in attempting to build a fortress at Ormuz. This, according to Almeida, was the head and front of Albuquerque's offending. It has been said that Almeida's policy was opposed to the building of many fortresses in the East, on the ground that it would not be possible to garrison them. He was afraid of the vast schemes of Albuquerque, and wrote to the King, alleging that Albuquerque had disobeyed orders by his conduct at Ormuz. Almeida's opposition to the policy of Albuquerque was increased by a personal grievance owing to the news which arrived in 1508, that Albuquerque was his destined successor at the close of three years of government. When, therefore, Albuquerque reached Cannanore, in December 1508, he found that the Viceroy was prejudiced against him and had received the mutinous captains with honour; and on Albuquerque's requesting the Viceroy to hand over the government to him, Almeida replied that his term did not expire till January 1509, and that he desired to defeat the Egyptian fleet of Emir Husain and to wreak vengeance for the death of his son, Dom Lourenço. Albuquerque acknowledged the force of these arguments, and retired to Cochin, where he remained inactive until Almeida's return, in March 1509, after the great victory off Diu.

Albuquerque again demanded that Almeida should resign the government to him. But the Viceroy, influenced by João da Nova and the other captains, who had good cause to fear Albuquerque's anger, persistently refused. They drew up a requisition to the Viceroy, which they got signed by many other officers, stating that Affonso de Albuquerque 'was a man of great inaptitude, and covetous, and of no sense, and one who knew not how to govern anything, much less so great a charge as the Empire of India.'[9] The Viceroy received this petition favourably. In August, 1509, he ordered Albuquerque to be imprisoned at Cannanore; he had a regular indictment in ninety-six counts drawn up against him; he declared his intention of sending him to Portugal in chains; and he tried to induce Diogo Lopes de Sequeira, who had just arrived from Portugal, to take over the government of India. So great was the Viceroy's wrath against Albuquerque that he gave orders for the destruction of all the houses in which Albuquerque had lived at Cochin, and took out of them everything that was to be found there; for he said that it was a case of treason, and very necessary that Albuquerque should be punished with rigour.

Matters remained in this state for two months, and the native princes on the Malabar coast, especially the Rájá of Cochin, were at a loss to understand the causes of these quarrels, for it had been a proud boast of the Portuguese that they would obey even a cabin boy who held the King's commission. The hopes of the Zamorin of Calicut began to revive, and it was fortunate for the Portuguese that, in October 1509, a fresh fleet arrived at Cannanore, under the command of Dom Fernão de Coutinho, Marshal of Portugal. This powerful nobleman was a relative of Albuquerque, and at once released him from custody. With Albuquerque on board, the Marshal sailed to Cochin, and he insisted that, in compliance with the royal mandate, Albuquerque should be immediately recognised as Governor of

[8] Albuquerque's *Commentaries,* vol. i. p. 206.

[9] Albuquerque's *Commentaries,* vol. ii. p. 33.

India.

Dom Francisco de Almeida saw that it was necessary for him to yield. He handed over the government on November 5 to Albuquerque, and on November 10, 1509, he left Cochin. His murder by savages at Saldanha Bay has been already noticed, and it is sad to have to narrate that he died without having been reconciled to his successor in the government of India. The *Commentaries* of Albuquerque imply that it was Albuquerque's fault that a reconciliation was not made, but, considering his conduct towards his greatest enemy, João da Nova, this does not seem to be probable; for it is written:—

> 'João da Nova died at Cochin in July 1509, so reduced in circumstances that he had no one to care for him; but Affonso de Albuquerque forgot all that he had been guilty of towards himself, and only held in memory that this man had been his companion in arms, and had helped him in all the troubles connected with the conquest of the kingdom of Ormuz like a gallant knight, and he ordered him to be buried at his own expense, with the usual display of torches, and himself accompanied the body to the grave, clad all in mourning, a thing the Viceroy would not have done.'[10]

[10] Albuquerque's *Commentaries,* vol. ii. p. 49.

CHAPTER III

THE RULE OF ALBUQUERQUE: THE CONQUEST OF GOA

It was on November 5, 1509, almost a year after he had reached India from his campaign in the Arabian seas, that Affonso de Albuquerque took up office as Governor and Captain-General of the Portuguese possessions in Asia. King Emmanuel had not conferred upon him the title of Viceroy, which had been held by his predecessor—probably because he had no right to the prefix Dom, or Lord. His powers, however, were as great as those exercised by Dom Francisco de Almeida, and he received a special patent granting him authority to confer *Moradias,* or palace pensions, for services rendered. There can be no doubt that during the months in which he had been kept out of his office by the intrigues of his enemies with the Viceroy Almeida, Albuquerque had carefully considered the state of affairs in India, for he struck the keynotes of his future policy immediately after taking up office.

The state of Southern India, and especially of the Malabar coast, was at this time very favourable to the aspirations of the Portuguese. The Hindu Rájás, with the exception of the Zamorin of Calicut, were greatly opposed to the monopoly by the Moplas of the commerce of their dominions. These Arab traders were as completely foreigners to the races of Southern India as the Portuguese themselves. They made proselytes to their religion, as the Portuguese afterwards endeavoured to do, but the Muhammadan converts were not favourably regarded either by the Rájás or their Bráhman ministers.

The most important ruler in Southern India was the Rájá of Vijayanagar or Narsingha. His power was still great, but it was threatened by the Muhammadan dynasties established in the Deccan, which eventually destroyed the power of the Vijayanagar kingdom at the battle of Tálikot in 1565. But when Albuquerque took up his office the Hindu kingdom was still powerful, and it might have been able with the assistance of the Portuguese to resist the advance of the Muhammadans.

The Portuguese felt none of the hatred which they showed to the disciples of Islám towards the Hindus. They had found to their great delight that the Christian religion flourished on the Malabar coast, and that the native Christians[11] were a prosperous and thriving community. They inclined to believe that the Hindus or Krishna-worshippers believed in a form of Christianity. The grounds for their be-

[11] On the early history of Christianity in India, see Hunter's *Indian Empire,* chapter ix, pp. 229-241.

lief were very slight, but sufficient to impress ardent Christians like Albuquerque himself. One of the first designs of the great Governor was to strike up a cordial alliance with the Hindu rulers. The friendship which the Rájá of Cochin had consistently shown to the Europeans gave him confidence, and one of his earliest measures was to send a Franciscan friar, Frei Luis, on a special embassy to the Rájá of Vijayanagar. The aim of this embassy was to induce the Rájá to attack the Zamorin of Calicut by land while the Portuguese attacked him by sea, but there was also a general desire expressed to make an alliance with the Rájá.

Frei Luis was directed to state in the name of Albuquerque:

> 'The King of Portugal commands me to render honour and willing service to all the Gentile Kings of this land and of the whole of Malabar, and that they are to be well treated by me, neither am I to take their ships nor their merchandise; but I am to destroy the Moors [Muhammadans], with whom I wage incessant war, as I know he also does; wherefore I am prepared and ready to help him with the fleets and armies of the King, my Lord, whensoever and as often as he shall desire me to do so; and I likewise, for my part, expect that he will help us with his army, towns, harbours, and munitions, and with everything that I may require from his kingdom; and the ships which navigate to his ports may pass safely throughout all the Indian sea, and receive honour and good treatment at the hands of the fleets and fortresses of the King of Portugal.'

Albuquerque goes on to say—

> 'And so I intend to drive out of Calicut the Moors, who are the people that furnish the Zamorin with all the revenue that he requires for the expenses of war, and after this is over I shall give my attention forthwith to the affairs of Goa, wherein I can help in the war against the King of the Deccan.'

Albuquerque then adds that Ormuz now belongs to the King of Portugal, and that—

> 'the horses of Ormuz shall not be consigned except to Baticala [Bhatkal] or to any other port he [the Rájá of Vijayanagar] pleases to point out where he can have them, and shall not go to the King of the Deccan, who is a Moor and his enemy.'[12]

These instructions make evident the attitude of Albuquerque, his desire to earn the friendship of Hindu rulers and his unrelenting enmity to all Muhammadans. He had not the absurd notion which Almeida attributed to him of desiring to establish a direct Portuguese rule all over India. He wished rather to pose as the destroyer of Muhammadanism and the liberator of the natives. In return for this service Portugal was to control the commerce of India with Europe. The attitude is not very different from that adopted by the English 300 years later, and it is a remarkable conception for a statesman at the very beginning of the sixteenth cen-

[12] Instructions to Frei Luis; Albuquerque's *Commentaries,* vol. ii. pp. 74-77.

tury.

Before however Albuquerque was able to combine operations with the Hindu Rájá of Narsingha he was forced, against his better judgment, to make an immediate attack unaided upon Calicut. Dom Fernão de Coutinho, the Marshal, insisted on this expedition against the Zamorin, on the ground that the King had ordered him to destroy Calicut before he returned to Portugal. The prudent Albuquerque endeavoured to dissuade the Marshal, but the headstrong young nobleman insisted on having his way. The entire military force of the Portuguese in India sailed for Calicut, and on Jan. 4, 1510, a landing was effected in front of the city. Albuquerque desired that a halt should then be made, as the men were very wearied, and could not bear the weight of their arms by reason of the great heat,—but in vain. He found himself forced to comply with the wishes of his impetuous relative, but he did his best to assure a safe retreat from the disaster, which he foresaw, by ordering Dom Antonio de Noronha, after burning the ships in the port, to remain in reserve with 300 men. Albuquerque then proceeded to follow the Marshal, who was rapidly making his way towards the Zamorin's palace. As the Marshal moved forward—

> 'There came against him twenty or thirty Nairs, armed with swords and shields, shouting aloud in their accustomed manner. When he caught sight of them coming against him he began to chuckle, and said to Gaspar Pereira, who was close beside him:—"Is this your Calicut that you terrify us all with in Portugal?" Gaspar Pereira replied that he would think differently before long; for he would wager that, if they could that day penetrate to the houses of the Zamorin, those little naked blacks would give them trouble enough. The Marshal replied:—"This is not the kind of people who will give me any trouble."[13]

The Portuguese vanguard under the Marshal managed to reach the Zamorin's palace, but the men soon scattered to plunder and got into disorder. They burnt the palace, but were hotly attacked by the Nairs when they endeavoured to retreat. More than eighty of the Portuguese were killed as they retired, including the Marshal and ten or twelve of the principal officers. Albuquerque himself was wounded, and all the invaders would probably have been cut to pieces but for the gallant conduct of the reserve under the command of Dom Antonio de Noronha. After this repulse, which was the most serious the Portuguese had sustained in India, Albuquerque returned to Cochin.

It is interesting to compare the account of this attack on Calicut, as given by Sheikh Zín-ud-dín in his historical work called the *Tohfut-ul-mujahideen*, which was written in the sixteenth century:—

> 'Now on Thursday, the 22nd day of the month of Ramzan, in the year of the Hejira 915, the Franks made a descent upon Calicut, committing great devastation and burning the Jama Mosque which was built by Nakuz Miscal; and they attacked also

[13] Albuquerque's *Commentaries*, vol. ii. p. 67.

> the palace of the Zamorin, hoping to obtain possession of it, as that prince was absent, being engaged in war in a distant part of his dominions. But the Nairs that had been left behind at Calicut, having united against these invaders, made an assault upon them, and succeeded in ejecting them from the palace, killing at the same time nearly 500 of their party; a great number also were drowned, and the few that escaped were saved by flying on board their vessels; having been entirely defeated in their designs by the permission of God Most High. Now, both before this time and after it, they made various descents upon the dominions of the Zamorin, burning in these attacks in all nearly fifty vessels that were lying near his shores, and conferring martyrdom upon upwards of seventy of the faithful.'[14]

After this serious disaster, which seemed an evil omen for Albuquerque's governorship, the great captain returned to Cochin to be healed of his wounds. Sickness however could not repress his energies, and he soon equipped his fleet afresh and took on board 1000 Portuguese soldiers. With this fleet he intended to sail to the Red Sea. Duarte de Lemos, who had succeeded him as Captain of the Ethiopian and Arabian Seas, earnestly implored the Governor to bring him help at once, alleging that his ships were rotten and unable to defend the island and fortress of Socotra. Albuquerque was well acquainted with King Emmanuel's desire to put an end to the Muhammadan commerce by way of the Red Sea. It was the notion which he had himself advocated to the King, and its execution was one of the principal aims of his policy. He desired also to return to Ormuz in order to punish the Minister, Cogeatar, and firmly establish Portuguese influence in the Persian Gulf. He therefore left Cochin with twenty-three ships on Feb. 10, 1510, and on his way to the island of Anchediva [Anjidiv], whence he intended to start for Arabia, he anchored off the port of Mergeu [Mirján]. He there considered an alternative scheme of campaign, namely, to attack Goa, for it was suggested to him by a native pirate or corsair captain, named Timoja or Timmaya, that it was a particularly suitable time for a sudden attack upon that central port.

This man played a most important part in the history of Portuguese conquest in India. He is reported to have been a Muhammadan by Correa, and, more correctly, a Hindu in the *Commentaries* of Albuquerque. The first Portuguese captain who had relations with this pirate was Dom Vasco da Gama during his second voyage to India in 1502. Correa says that certain ships—

> 'were *fustas* of thieves, which, with oars and sails, got into a river called Onor (Honáwar), where there was a Moor who equipped them, named Timoja.... This Moor committed great robberies at sea upon all that he fell in with, and this Moor was a foreigner and paid part of the plunder to the King of Gersoppa, who was ruler of the country.'[15]

[14] *Tohfut-ul-mujahideen,* translated by Lieut. M. J. Rowlandson for the Oriental Translation Fund, 1833; pp. 97-99.

[15] *The Three Voyages of Vasco da Gama,* translated from Correa's *Lendas da India:* Hak-

Vasco da Gama had on this information burnt various ships belonging to Timoja. But the native chieftain seems to have borne the Portuguese no ill feeling for this, and entered into very friendly relations with Dom Francisco de Almeida, the Viceroy. He had written to Albuquerque before the ill-fated attack upon Calicut, begging the Governor to direct his fleet against Goa, and while Albuquerque was on his way on this occasion to the Red Sea, Timoja arrived to parley with him at Mergeu.

> 'This man,' it is said in the *Commentaries* of Albuquerque, 'was a Hindu by birth, very obedient to the interests of the King of Portugal; and being a man of low origin had, as a corsair, raised himself to a position of great honour.'[16]

He informed Albuquerque that the Lord of Goa was dead, and that great dissensions had arisen among his nobles, which left a very favourable opportunity for an attack on the city. The Governor called a council of his captains, and after considering Timoja's arguments it was unanimously resolved to put off the expedition to the Red Sea and to attack Goa.

The capture of Goa is perhaps the most important event of Albuquerque's administration, and the reasons which led to it deserve special consideration. The island of Goa was situated upon the Malabar coast about half way between Bombay and Cape Comorin. It was formed by the mouths of two rivers and was thus easily fitted for defence. At the time of its capture there was a bar at the mouth of the harbour, allowing in full flood ships drawing three fathoms of water to enter, and the anchorage inside was absolutely safe. It had always been the centre of an important trade, and was visited by merchants of many nationalities. By some authorities its trade is represented as larger than that of Calicut, and at any rate it was but slightly inferior. From its situation, and the ease with which it could be fortified, it was well fitted to become the capital of the Portuguese in India.

Albuquerque's ideas, as has already been said, differed from those of Almeida in one important particular. Albuquerque wished to establish a real Portuguese empire, which should rest upon the possession of Portuguese colonies owning the direct sway of the King of Portugal. Almeida thought it sufficient to command the sea, and that the only land stations should be a few factories in commercial cities, defended by fortifications against all assaults. Almeida therefore was quite satisfied that the fortresses he had built at Cannanore, Cochin, and Quilon were all that was needed; but Albuquerque considered it derogatory for the Portuguese to have their headquarters on sufferance in the capitals of native rulers. He felt it would be impolitic to attack the Rájás who had been friendly with the Portuguese, and he therefore resolved to establish a Portuguese capital in another part of the Malabar coast quite independent of the existing factories. Geographically also he considered Cochin as too far south for the effective maintenance of the Portuguese power in India, and he therefore looked out for a more central situation. Goa seemed to offer just what he wanted, a good harbour and a central situation, while its capture would not offend any of the native allies of the Portuguese.

luyt Soc. 1869, p. 309.

[16] Albuquerque's *Commentaries*, vol. ii. p. 81.

There was another political consideration which also weighed with Albuquerque. Hitherto the chief enemies of the Portuguese had been Muhammadan merchants, who had, in the instance of Calicut, induced the Hindu ruler to take the offensive. But Goa was the actual possession of a Muhammadan ruler, and its conquest would strike a direct blow at the growing Muhammadan power in India.

Goa belonged to various Hindu dynasties until the early part of the fourteenth century, when it was conquered by the Muhammadan Nawáb of Honáwar. In 1367, however, the Hindu minister of Harihara, Rájá of Vijayanagar, reconquered the city, and it remained a part of the great Hindu kingdom of Southern India for more than seventy years. In 1440 the inhabitants of the old city of Goa attained their independence, and soon after founded the new city of Goa in another part of the island. Its trade, especially in horses, imported from Ormuz, grew rapidly, and in 1470 it was conquered by the Muhammadan King of the Deccan, Muhammad Sháh II. So great was the monarch's joy at the conquest, that it is stated in Ferishta that he ordered 'the march of triumph to be beaten for seven days.'

In 1472 the Hindu Rájá of Belgáum, and in 1481 the Rájá of Vijayanagar made unsuccessful attacks upon Goa. Amid the later troubles of the great Báhmani kingdom of the Deccan, which occurred on the death of Muhammad Sháh II, Goa fell to the lot of the Muhammadan kingdom of Bijápur. The founder of this kingdom was Yusaf Adil Sháh, a son of Amurad II, Sultan of the Ottoman Turks. That prince had a most romantic history. He was rescued by his mother from being put to death with his brothers on the accession to the throne of Muhammad II. He was secretly delivered over to a merchant of Sava in Persia who educated him. He took the name of Savái from the place of his education, and is always called by the Portuguese historians the Sabaio or Çabaio, or the Hidalcão, a version of Adil Khán. He came to India as a slave, but he rose rapidly from a simple soldier to the command of the royal body-guard of the Báhmani kings, and was eventually made Governor of Bijápur. In 1489 he was crowned King of Bijápur, and under his rule Goa, which formed part of his dominions, greatly increased in wealth.

Yusaf Adil Sháh erected many fine buildings, including a magnificent palace at Goa. He even thought, it is said, of making it his capital, and there can be no doubt that he vastly augmented its prosperity. But his government was oppressive to the Hindu population; he doubled the taxes, and by favouring his own creed made himself hated by all his Hindu subjects. When Timoja pressed Albuquerque to attack Goa, the Muhammadan Governor, whose name, Málik Yusaf Gurgi, is rendered by the Portuguese Melique Çufegurgij, had made himself especially obnoxious from the cruelties wreaked by his Turkish garrison on the citizens. Yusaf Adil Sháh was not dead, as Timoja told Albuquerque, but was absent in the interior, and the time was really favourable for a sudden assault. A Jogi or Hindu ascetic had prophesied that a foreign people coming from a distant land would conquer Goa, and the inhabitants were therefore ready to surrender the city without much opposition to the Portuguese.

Influenced by these considerations, and the arguments of Timoja, Albuquerque altered the direction of his armament and cast anchor off Goa harbour. On March 1, 1510, Dom Antonio de Noronha, Albuquerque's gallant nephew, crossed the bar with the ships' boats of the Portuguese fleet, two galleys commanded by Diogo Fernandes de Beja and Simão de Andrade, and the *fustas* or native boats of Timoja, and stormed the fortress of Panjim, which is situated at the entrance to the harbour. The ships then entered, and on the 3rd of March the city of Goa surrendered without making any defence.[17] The Governor for the Muhammadan King and his soldiers had fled with such haste that many fugitives were drowned in crossing the rivers. Albuquerque entered the city in triumph, and proceeded to the palace of Yusaf Adil Sháh, where his first measure was to appoint Dom Antonio de Noronha to be Captain of the city. He was hailed with shouts of welcome by the people, who showered on him flowers made of gold and silver. The Governor at once prepared to strengthen the defences of the city; the ships' crews were brought ashore, and both Portuguese and natives were set to work to build a strong wall round the city, and a citadel.

Albuquerque was well aware of the effect his conquest would have upon the minds of other native sovereigns. He received ambassadors from the Rájá of Vijayanagar, who plainly hinted that their master expected Goa would be made over to him. He also received ambassadors from the King of Ormuz and from Sháh Ismáil of Persia. These Muhammadan potentates had despatched their ambassadors to the King of Bijápur to incite him to join in a general war against the Portuguese. But when they found Albuquerque in possession of the city of Goa, they adroitly changed the purpose of their missions, and made overtures to him instead. Albuquerque received them with fair words. He had not abandoned his schemes against Ormuz, but he desired to stand well with Ismáil Sháh. He thoroughly understood the exact position of Ismáil, the greatest of the Sufi Sháhs of Persia, whom the Portuguese always called the Sophy, and that Ismáil belonged to the Shiah sect of Muhammadans, and as such was the enemy of the Turks, who were orthodox Muhammadans.

Albuquerque nominated Ruy Gomes as ambassador to Ismáil Sháh, and the instructions which he took with him are very significant of Albuquerque's wide range of policy. Ruy Gomes never reached the Persian Court, being poisoned upon the way at Ormuz, but part of his instructions deserve quotation:

> 'You shall tell Sháh Ismáil how my Lord the King will be pleased to come to an understanding and alliance with him, and will assist him in his war against the Sultan; and that I, in his name and on his behalf, offer him the fleet and army and artillery which I have with me, and the fortresses, towns, and lordships, which the King of Portugal holds in India, and I will give him all this same help against the Turk.'[18]

In his letter to the Sháh, Albuquerque lays weight also upon the advantages which might be derived from an alliance with the Portuguese:

---

[17] The dates of the first capture of Goa are given differently. The *Commentaries* of Albuquerque gives March 3, vol. ii. pp. 88-92; Correa, *Lendas da India,* vol. ii p. 59, says March 1. Barros, Decade II, Book V, chapter 3, ed. of 1777, pp. 464, 465; Castanheda, vol. iii. ed. of 1833, p. 30; and Faria e Sousa, *Asia Portugueza,* ed. of 1666, vol. i. p. 137, all fix February 17.

[18] Instructions to Ruy Gomes; Albuquerque's *Commentaries,* vol. ii. pp. 114-118.

> 'I believe that with small trouble,' he says, 'you must gain the Lordship of the city of Cairo, and all his kingdom and dependencies.... If God grant that this intercourse and alliance be ratified, come you with all your power against the city of Cairo and the lands of the Grand Sultan which are on the borders of your own, and the King my Lord shall pass over to Jerusalem and gain from him all the land on that side.'[19]

These ideas deserve notice both as illustrating the grandiose conceptions of Albuquerque, and his skill in taking advantage of dissensions among the foes of the Christian religion. To him doubtless it mattered not whether the Muhammadans he attacked were Shiahs or Sunís—all alike were infidels; but he was perfectly ready to make use of the one sect against the other. He calmly put on one side the demand of the Persian ambassador that the Shiah form of Muhammadanism should be proclaimed in Goa, and that Ismáil Sháh's money should pass current, but he nevertheless dismissed the ambassador with fair words.

Albuquerque was soon distracted from questions of general policy by the advance of the King of Bijápur upon the island of Goa with 60,000 men. As had happened at Ormuz, his captains did not share his views. They declared it to be impossible to defend Goa, and strongly resented being engaged in the hard work of building walls instead of in the more lucrative business of collecting cargoes for Portugal. The news of the advance of Yusaf Adil Sháh increased the reluctance of the captains to remain, but Albuquerque nevertheless refused to evacuate Goa. The Muhammadan king made overtures to him and promised to cede to the Portuguese any other port in his dominions except Goa, and it was even hinted that Goa itself would be given up, if Albuquerque would surrender Timoja, who was looked on as a traitor to his country. This proposition it need hardly be said was rejected with scorn. Eventually, whether from the unwillingness of the Portuguese captains or from sheer impossibility of defence, Yusaf Adil Sháh's army made its way into the island of Goa on May 17, 1510. The Portuguese at first hoped to hold the citadel of Goa; but finding the position untenable, Albuquerque withdrew his men to their ships, after setting fire to the arsenal and beheading 150 of the principal Muhammadan prisoners whom he had in his possession.

He then dropped down the river with his fleet, but was unable to cross the bar owing to the state of the weather. For nearly three months the Portuguese fleet remained at anchor at the mouth of the harbour of Goa. It was one of the most critical periods in Albuquerque's life, and during it he exhibited the highest qualities of a commander. At their anchorage, the Portuguese found themselves exposed to the fire of the King of Bijápur's artillery, mounted in the castle of Panjim, which had been abandoned after the capture of Goa. Albuquerque therefore decided to make a night attack upon this position. The fight was a fierce one. Several of the Portuguese were killed, and it was with difficulty that the garrison was expelled on June 14, 1510.

This successful expedition was followed by another, marred only by the death of the young hero of the fleet, Dom Antonio de Noronha. News had reached Al-

[19] Letter to Sháh Ismáil; Albuquerque's *Commentaries*, vol. ii. pp. 111-114.

buquerque that Yusaf Adil Sháh had prepared a number of fire-ships, which he intended to send down the river to set fire to the Portuguese fleet. He therefore sent his boats to reconnoitre. They reached the dockyard, but in endeavouring to cut out one of the enemy's ships, which was still on the stocks, Dom Antonio de Noronha was mortally wounded. He died on July 8, and, in the words of the *Commentaries,*

> 'There was not a single person in the whole of the fleet who was not deeply affected, but especially his uncle, in that he had been deprived of him at a season when he most needed his personal assistance, his advice, and his knightly example.... He was a very brave cavalier, and never found himself placed in any position which caused him any fear. He was very virtuous, very godfearing, and very truthful. He was found side by side with Affonso de Albuquerque in every one of the troubles which up to the hour of his death had come upon him. He died at the age of twenty-four years, four having elapsed since he set out from Portugal with his uncle in the fleet of Tristão da Cunha.'[20]

At no time indeed was Albuquerque more in need of help and advice; his fleet was blockaded in the harbour and stricken with famine; his men deserted in numbers and became renegades; and his captains were in almost open mutiny. It was at this time that he ordered the execution of one of his soldiers, a young Portuguese fidalgo named Ruy Dias, which is treated by the poet Camoens as the chief blot upon the great commander's fame. It was reported to Albuquerque that Ruy Dias had been in the habit of visiting the Muhammadan women whom he had brought with him as hostages from Goa. There is no doubt that through these women information was conveyed to the enemy of the state of affairs in the Portuguese fleet, and Albuquerque therefore directed Pedro de Alpoem, the *Ouvidor*—that is, the Auditor of Portuguese India, who performed the duties of Chief Magistrate—to try Ruy Dias, and he was condemned to be hanged. While the execution was being carried out, certain of the captains rowed up and down among the ships crying 'Murder,' and one of them, Francisco de Sá, went so far as to cut through the rope with which Ruy Dias was being hanged, with his sword. Albuquerque at once determined to maintain discipline. The execution of Ruy Dias was completed, and Francisco de Sá, with three captains, Jorge Fogaça, Fernão Peres de Andrade and Simão de Andrade, were put in irons.

The extent of the suffering from sickness and starvation in the fleet was made known to Yusaf Adil Sháh by deserters, and that monarch, with true chivalry, offered to send provisions to the Portuguese, stating that he wished to conquer them not by starvation but by the sword. Albuquerque resolved to receive no such assistance from his enemies. He collected on board his own ship all the wine and food that was left, which was being kept for the use of the sick, and displayed it to the messengers of the King of Bijápur. Throughout this difficult period the two generals vied with each other in generosity. One fact is particularly worthy of notice. Yusaf Adil Sháh at the request of Albuquerque refused to allow the Portu-

[20] Albuquerque's *Commentaries,* vol. ii. pp. 180, 181.

guese deserters, who had joined him, to continue going down to the banks of the harbour to incite other soldiers and sailors to desert. At last in August, 1510, the weather changed; it became once more possible to cross the bar, and the Portuguese fleet sailed away from Goa. But Albuquerque was not a man to be depressed by one failure. He had resolved that Goa should be the capital of Portuguese India, and he never rested until he had attained his end.

It was on August 15 that Albuquerque sailed out of Goa harbour, and to his great joy the first sight he saw was a Portuguese squadron of four ships which had just arrived from Portugal under the command of Diogo Mendes de Vasconcellos. The Governor stopped for a time at the anchorage of Anchediva Island, and then proceeded to Honáwar (Onor), where he had an interview with Timoja, who had been able to leave Goa harbour with his light native galleys before the larger Portuguese ships. Timoja gave him information that Yusaf Adil Sháh had left Goa for Bijápur three days after the departure of the Portuguese fleet, and also that directly the main Muhammadan army had gone the people in the neighbourhood of Goa had risen in insurrection. Timoja therefore pressed Albuquerque to make a second attack on Goa as soon as possible, which was exactly what the Portuguese commander had determined to do. Albuquerque then sailed south to Cannanore, where he was met by Duarte de Lemos, who had succeeded him as Captain of the Arabian Seas.

Duarte de Lemos told Albuquerque that his nephew, Dom Affonso de Noronha, had left Socotra in the previous April, and had never been heard of again, and the news of this loss increased his sorrow for the loss of his other nephew, Dom Antonio. Duarte de Lemos took advantage of his position as a Chief Captain to entreat Albuquerque to release the captains and other gentlemen whom he had imprisoned for insubordination in the harbour of Goa. Albuquerque accordingly released all except Jorge Fogaça, whom he regarded as the ringleader, and some of those to whom he showed clemency, notably the brothers Andrade, afterwards did him good service, and showed themselves worthy of his forgiveness.

While he was at Cannanore, Albuquerque received an ambassador from Mahmúd Sháh Begára, the Muhammadan King of Ahmadábád, informing him that Dom Affonso de Noronha's ship had been wrecked off the coast of Gujarát, and that, though Dom Affonso was drowned, most of his men were saved and were detained in custody. The mere fact that such an embassy was sent showed how far the fame of the great Portuguese captain had already extended.

During this period of waiting, two other squadrons joined Albuquerque under the command of Gonçalo de Sequeira and João Serrão, making the amount of reinforcements which had reached him during the year fourteen ships and 1500 Portuguese warriors. But his difficulties were not yet over. Two of these squadrons, those of Diogo Mendes and João Serrão, had been sent for the express purpose, the former of going to Malacca, the latter of exploring the Red Sea. These captains wished to depart at once on their several missions, and desired not to co-operate in a second attack on Goa. Gonçalo de Sequeira, on his part, declared that his ships were ships of burden and that it was his duty to load them with cargo for Portugal.

Albuquerque knew how eagerly King Emmanuel expected his merchant-ships, and, like Warren Hastings in later times, he was forced to subordinate his political aims to the commercial objects of his employer. He therefore sailed to Cochin, where he invested a new Rájá in the place of his deceased uncle and got ready the cargo for Portugal. But, though he yielded to Sequeira's representations, he insisted upon being accompanied to Goa by the squadrons of Diogo Mendes and João Serrão. Duarte de Lemos was greatly disgusted with this decision, and demanded leave to return to Portugal instead of to his station at the mouth of the Red Sea. Albuquerque acceded to his request, and placed him in command of the squadron of cargo-ships which was about to return to Portugal.

The combined Portuguese war-fleet then sailed to Honáwar, where Albuquerque was present at the marriage of his ally Timoja to a daughter of the Rájá of Gersoppa. Timoja pressed the Portuguese Governor to attack Goa as soon as possible. He informed him that Yusaf Adil Sháh had now gone so far into the interior that he would be unable to relieve the city, and also that the garrison of Goa consisted not of more than 4000 Turks and Persians under the command of a general named Rasúl Khán, whom the Portuguese called Roçalcão. Under these circumstances the Portuguese Governor resolved to attack, and in the beginning of November he sailed once more into the harbour of Goa with twenty-eight ships carrying 1700 soldiers, accompanied by a large number of native troops belonging to Timoja and the Rájá of Gersoppa.

On November 25, 1510, the Portuguese assaulted the city of Goa in three columns. Each was entirely successful; the Turks fought desperately, and at least half of them, or 2000 men, were killed. The Portuguese lost forty killed and 150 wounded. Many feats of valour on the part of the Portuguese warriors are related by different chroniclers, two of which deserve mention here, as they illustrate the chivalrous conduct of the Portuguese in those days. Perhaps the most striking is the story of Dom Jeronymo de Lima, a young nobleman, who had accompanied Almeida to India, and remained to serve under Albuquerque. He was mortally wounded at the storming of the gate of the fortress.

> 'And while he lay on the ground so severely struck that he could not survive, his brother, Dom João de Lima, who was wheeling round with others, came upon him; and when he beheld him in such a condition, with his head leaning against the wall, he exclaimed, with many tears, "What is this, brother? How art thou?" Dom Jeronymo replied, "I am on the point of finishing this journey, and I am glad, as it has pleased Our Lord to require this service of me, that it has been completed here in His service, and in that of the King of Portugal." Dom João de Lima desired to remain in company with him; but he said, "Brother, there is no time for you to remain with me; go and perform what is required of you. I will remain here and finish my days, for I have no longer any strength left." So Dom João de Lima left him and went on, following after the Moors; and when the fortress had been captured and the Moors driven out, he returned to seek after his brother, and

> found him already dead. I should be very glad to have been either one of the two brothers [the chronicler quaintly adds], but I know not how to decide which one of the two I most envy,—whether Dom João de Lima, because he went to fight where such another one as himself could be met with, or Dom Jeronymo de Lima, who did not desire to remedy his wounds, although they were mortal (it being a very natural thing for men to desire to live), but rather sought to advance his brother's honour, and would not consent to his remaining behind with him at a time when the other fidalgos and cavaliers were carrying on the fight with the Turks within the fortress. The decision of this I leave to those who read the lessons of this history; let them judge which of these two brothers best performed his obligations.'[21]

Another anecdote illustrates Albuquerque's personal admiration of warlike prowess. Manoel de Lacerda was wounded in the face by an arrow; but nevertheless he killed a mounted Turk, seized his horse, and continued to fight with the broken arrow fixed in his face and his armour covered with blood. At this moment the Turks rallied and attacked Lacerda's force with 500 men. Albuquerque, on receiving information of this resistance, came up with his reserve to the point of danger.

> 'As soon as Manoel de Lacerda beheld Affonso de Albuquerque, he dismounted his charger and presented it to him. When Affonso de Albuquerque saw him with his armour all smirched with blood, he embraced him and said, "Sir Manoel de Lacerda, I declare to you that I am greatly envious of you, and so would Alexander the Great have been, had he been here, for you look more gallant for an evening's rendezvous than the Emperor Aurelian."'[22]

The moment the victory was won, Affonso de Albuquerque gave thanks to God, and promised to erect a church in honour of St. Catherine, whose feast day is the 25th November, on the site of the gate which had been so hardly won. He also conferred the honour of knighthood upon some of the most distinguished of the younger soldiers, among whom were Frederico Fernandes, who had been the first man to enter the city, and Manoel da Cunha, a younger son of his former commander, Tristão da Cunha.

As soon as the Portuguese were in entire possession of Goa, Albuquerque directed that the Muhammadan population, men, women and children, should be put to the sword. This cruel butchery is far more to Albuquerque's discredit than the hanging of Ruy Dias, for which the poet Camoens so strongly condemns him. It is only partially justified by Albuquerque's belief that the Muhammadans of Goa had behaved treacherously towards him in the spring and had admitted Yusaf Adil Sháh into the island. It is more likely that it was mainly due to Albuquerque's crusading hatred against the religion of the Prophet. He also gave up

[21] Albuquerque's *Commentaries,* vol. iii. pp. 13, 14.
[22] Albuquerque's *Commentaries,* vol. iii. p. 12.

the city to plunder, and for three days his soldiers were occupied in the work of sacking it. He then set to work to repair the walls and ramparts, and especially to rebuild the citadel. His loss of the place in the spring made him particularly anxious to complete this work, and to set an example he himself did not hesitate to set his hands to it. When the citadel was completed he ordered a stone to be set up containing the names of all the captains who had served at the assault. But there was so much dissension as to the order in which the names should be engraved, every one desiring to be first, that eventually he placed on it only these words '*Lapidem quem reprobaverunt ædificantes'*—*the stone which the builders rejected.*[23]

It is curious to compare with the real history of Albuquerque's two occupations of Goa the account given by the Muhammadan historian in the *Tohfut-ul-mujahideen*, but it need hardly be said that the bribery to which he refers had no foundation in fact.

> 'Moreover,' writes the Sheikh Zín-ud-dín, 'the Franks having commenced hostilities against the inhabitants of Goa and captured that place, proceeded to take possession of it. Now this port was one of those that belonged to Adil Sháh (peace to his remains!); notwithstanding this, however, the Franks having seized upon it, made choice of it for their seat of government in India, proceeding to exercise rule over it. But Adil Sháh attacking these intruders, repulsed them; he in turn making it a rallying-place for Islámism. Subsequently the Franks (the curse of God rest on them!) made preparations for a second attack upon Goa, and proceeding against it with a vast armament and assaulting it, they at last captured it. It is said, however, that they bribed over to their interests some of its principal inhabitants, in which case its capture was not a feat of much difficulty; and the Franks on thus re-obtaining possession of Goa, hastened to construct around it extensive fortifications of vast height. After their acquisition of this place, their power became greatly increased, every day bringing some accession to it: for the Lord as he wills, so indeed does he bring to pass.'[24]

Albuquerque took Goa for the second time at a most favourable moment, for Yusaf Adil Sháh, his gallant enemy of the previous spring, died on December 5, 1510. His son, Ismáil Adil Sháh, who succeeded him, was a mere lad, and the governors of the different provinces of his kingdom soon began to show signs of rebellion. Under these circumstances Kamal Khán, the principal general and minister of the State of Bijápur, made, according to the Muhammadan historian Ferishta, an arrangement with the Portuguese, and consented to their retaining possession of Goa, on condition that they would be satisfied with the island and would not molest the adjoining districts. Albuquerque's *Commentaries* say nothing of this ar-

---

[23] According to Barros, Decade II, Book V, ch. 11, ed. of 1778, p. 558, and Correa, *Lendas da India,* vol. ii. p. 157; but in the *Commentaries,* vol. iii. p. 137, this anecdote is told of the building of the fortress at Malacca.

[24] *Tohfut-ul-mujahideen,* Rowlandson's translation, pp. 100-102.

rangement with Kamal Khán, but they contain a letter written by the Portuguese Governor to the youthful King of Bijápur directly after the second capture of Goa. The letter is both curious and characteristic.

> 'You must well know,' he wrote, 'how the Sabaio, your father, used to take the ships of Malabar out of the ports and harbours of the King, my Lord; wherefore it was that I was constrained to go against Goa, and take the city, and there it is that I am now occupied in building a very strong fortress. I wish most sincerely that your father had been living, that he might know me to be a man of my word: out of regard for him I shall be ever your friend, and I will assist you against the King of the Deccan and against your enemies; and I will cause all the horses that arrive here to be carried to your stations and your marts, in order that you may have possession of them. Fain would I that the merchants of your land would come with white stuffs and all manner of merchandize to this port, and take to yours in exchange merchandize of the sea, and of the land, and horses, and I will give them a safe conduct. If you wish for my friendship, let your messengers come to me with your communications, and I will send you others on my part, who shall convey to you my communications: if you will perform this which I write unto you, by my aid shall you be able to gain possession of much land, and become a great Lord among the Moors. Be desirous of performing this, for thus it shall be well with you, and you shall have great power; and for all that the Sabaio, your father, be dead, I will be your father and bring you up like a son.'[25]

The conquest of Goa had an immense effect upon all the sovereigns on the western side of India. Not only did the Muhammadan King of Ahmadábád send ambassadors to Albuquerque asking to make an alliance with him, but the Hindu Zamorin of Calicut, hitherto the principal foe of the Portuguese, also sued for peace. Albuquerque took a high hand with the latter; too much Portuguese blood had been shed in Calicut for him to desire a treaty of alliance. The only terms he would accept were that he should have permission to build a fortress in the very heart of Calicut commanding the harbour. As the Zamorin would not accept these terms, which would leave his capital and his commerce at the mercy of the Portuguese, the negotiations were broken off. With Mahmúd Sháh Begára, King of Ahmadábád, communications were carried on in a more friendly tone. The King promised to release the men who had been wrecked with Dom Affonso de Noronha, and ordered the Emir Husain to leave his dominions at once. He even offered the island of Diu as a site for a Portuguese fortress, but Albuquerque had not sufficient strength in India at that moment to accept the offer.

The conquest of Goa, both in its immediate and in its ultimate results, was one of the greatest achievements of Albuquerque's governorship. It gave the Portuguese a commercial and political capital; it showed the neighbouring rulers, both

[25] Albuquerque's *Commentaries,* vol. iii. pp. 20, 21.

Hindu and Muhammadan, that the Portuguese intended to remain on the Malabar coast as a governing power, and not simply, like the Arab Moplas, as a commercial community; and the gallantry shown in the final assault, as well as during the sojourn of the fleet in the harbour of Goa, proved to the people of India that a new warrior race had come amongst them. Its ultimate results are quite as important. Goa, by the policy of the successors of Albuquerque, concentrated the whole trade of the Malabar coast. To increase the prosperity of Goa the earlier centres of trade, such as Calicut and Cochin and Quilon, were purposely deprived of their freedom to buy and sell; Goa became the seat of the Viceroys and Governors of Portuguese India; its wealth passed into a proverb; and though the glory of Golden Goa lasted but a century,[26] it was during that century one of the most splendid cities on the face of the earth.

[26] On the later history of Goa, see Hunter's *Imperial Gazetteer of India,* ed. 1885, vol. v. pp. 101-105.

CHAPTER IV

THE RULE OF ALBUQUERQUE (CONTINUED): THE CONQUEST OF MALACCA AND RELIEF OF GOA

Albuquerque's first thought after the completion of the fortifications of Goa was to provide for its future government. He determined to leave the place with the bulk of his forces as soon as possible, for the sacked and partially burnt city was unable to supply sufficient provisions for all his men. He accordingly appointed Rodrigo Rebello to be Captain of the fortress of Goa, Francisco Pantoja to be Alcaide-Mor or Chief Constable, with the right of succeeding Rebello in case of accident, and Francisco Corvinel to be Factor. It was more difficult to find a governor for the island as distinguished from the city. This post he had conferred, after the first capture, on his ally Timoja, but he now selected a celebrated Hindu captain, who was much respected by the Hindu population, called by the Portuguese Merlão or Milrrhão, probably versions of Malhár Ráo. This man was the brother of the Rájá of Honáwar and had won distinction by defending Goa against the Muhammadans in former days. He agreed to pay a sum equivalent to about £30,000 a year for the privilege of governing the island of Goa. Under the command of Rodrigo Rebello, Albuquerque left 400 Portuguese soldiers, together with plenty of artillery and ammunition, for the defence of the fortress.

The Governor then resolved to set out at once for the Red Sea. King Emmanuel, whose main idea it was to close this route to commerce, had directed him to dismantle the fortress on the island of Socotra, owing to the difficulty of getting provisions, and to occupy Aden instead. When this decision became known, Diogo Mendes, who had been specially ordered to Malacca, murmured loudly, and declared his intention of leaving the Governor and at once departing with his squadron westwards. Albuquerque expostulated with him; he pointed out that four ships could not conquer the Malays, and argued that their treatment of the first Portuguese squadron showed that they would not permit the Portuguese to open up trade without first being defeated. He even showed Diogo Mendes a letter which had arrived from the Portuguese Factor left at Malacca, stating that he and his comrades were kept as prisoners. He promised that, as soon as the King's commands with regard to the Red Sea had been carried out, he would himself proceed with a powerful fleet to the Malay Peninsula, and firmly establish Portuguese influence in that quarter.

Diogo Mendes felt the force of these arguments, but the master of his flagship,

Dinis Cerniche, would not agree, and setting sail crossed the bar of Goa harbour on his way out. The Governor at once sent a ship, under Jaymé Teixeira, with orders to make Mendes return by any means in his power. Since the master would not shorten sail, the ship was fired on and forced to return by the destruction of its main yard. Albuquerque forgave Mendes, but ordered Cerniche to be executed, which sentence was not carried out, but the master was instead sent back to Portugal in custody. Nevertheless the persistency of Mendes and his men seems to have greatly influenced Albuquerque, for finding in Feb. 1511, when he sailed out of Goa harbour, that it was impossible to sail westward owing to the monsoon, he resolved to make his way to Malacca. He first sailed to Cochin, where he appointed Manoel de Lacerda to be Captain of the Indian Sea with supreme authority, and he directed that Lacerda's orders should be obeyed as if they were his own.

Albuquerque's conquest of Malacca ranks second in importance among his great feats of arms to the capture of Goa. It gave the Portuguese the complete command of the spice trade, and eventually of the Chinese and Japanese trade. It struck the final blow at the Muhammadan commercial routes to Europe. Hitherto the Portuguese had only secured the monopoly of the Indian trade, and Muhammadan vessels, largely manned by Arabs, still collected the produce of Bengal and Burma, of Sumatra and the Spice Islands, of Siam and China, at the great commercial port of the Malay Peninsula. Albuquerque resolved to check this trade by holding the mouth of the Red Sea, but it seemed to him of even more efficacy to seize upon the headquarters of the trade itself.

The city of Malacca, with its splendid harbour, was the capital of a wealthy Muhammadan Sultan. This man's ancestors were said to have come from the neighbouring island of Java, and to have been converted to Islám some 200 years before. Constant war had been waged between the Kings of Siam, who formerly ruled the whole peninsula, and the Javanese immigrants; but the latter had held their own, and by a wise encouragement of commerce had become very wealthy and powerful. The trade of Malacca with India is said by the Portuguese chroniclers to have been largely in the hands of merchants from Gujarát, and when the Portuguese conquered the city it was inhabited by men of nearly every Eastern race, Hindus from both sides of India, Arabs, Chinese and Javanese. It is mentioned that on their arrival they found, among other officers, four men holding the title of Xabandar (Sháh-i-Bandar) or Captain of the Port. These four men are expressly stated to have been governors of different districts, and they are said to have belonged to four different nationalities and to rule over the Chinese, the Javanese, the Gujarátís and the Bengalís respectively. This division probably fairly indicates the chief nationalities of the merchants of Malacca.

Malacca was first visited by a European squadron on September 11, 1509. Diogo Lopes de Sequeira had been despatched by King Emmanuel with instructions to explore the island of Madagascar, and afterwards to proceed to the Malay Peninsula, which was well known to the Portuguese king by its classical name of the Golden Chersonese. The arrival of Sequeira in India during the viceroyalty of Almeida has been already noticed, and mention has been made of the Viceroy's wish that he should take over the government in the place of Albuquerque. Sequeira declined this offer and sailed for the Malay Peninsula with his squadron of five ships, but he so far complied with the Viceroy's wishes as to carry with him the chief friends of Albuquerque, and notably his most constant supporter, Ruy de Araujo.

Sequeira visited Sumatra, and safely reached Malacca. He was favourably received at first by the Sultan, and sent ashore Ruy de Araujo to fill the perilous post of Factor. As a lucrative trade seemed likely to spring up, the Portuguese captain proceeded to land a large quantity of goods together with several Portuguese clerks. But as usual the Muhammadan merchants soon showed their jealousy of the Portuguese, as they had always done on the Malabar coast. The Bendara, or native Prime Minister of Malacca, listened to the suggestions of the Moslem merchants, and formed a plan to destroy the whole Portuguese squadron. It was resolved to invite all the officers to a grand banquet at which they should be suddenly murdered, and in their absence it was believed that the ships might be easily taken. A Javanese woman, who had fallen in love with one of the Portuguese, swam out to their ships and gave warning of the plot. The Portuguese officers in consequence declined to land, and as soon as their determination was made known, the Malays set upon the factory, and made Ruy de Araujo and about twenty men whom he had with him prisoners.

They defended themselves gallantly, but Sequeira made no effort to assist them, and sailed away out of the harbour. He was obliged before leaving the peninsula to burn two of his ships for want of men to navigate them, and with the other three he made his way to India. When he reached the Malabar coast and touched at Caecoulão (Káyenkolam), he heard that the Marshal had placed Albuquerque in power, and that Almeida had departed. Sequeira, fearing the vengeance of Albuquerque, at once set sail for Portugal, sending his other two vessels under the command of Nuno Vaz de Castello-Branco to join the Governor at Cochin. It was to wreak vengeance on the Sultan of Malacca and to open up trade there that the squadron of Diogo Mendes de Vasconcellos had been sent from Portugal in 1510; but, as has been related, in spite of the captain's wishes, he and his men had been detained by Albuquerque to take part in the second capture of Goa.

Ruy de Araujo wrote a pathetic letter to Albuquerque, describing the manner in which he and his companions were treated. He told his friend that there were nineteen Portuguese alive at Malacca, who had been greatly tortured to make them turn Muhammadans. He also said that they had been very kindly treated by a Hindu merchant, named Ninachatu, who had secured the means for the despatch of the letter. He begged Albuquerque, for the love of God, to keep them in remembrance, and rescue them out of their captivity; and he also requested that the kindness of the Hindu merchant should not be made known for fear that the Moslems of the Malabar coast should give information to their co-religionists at Malacca.

It may well be imagined that Albuquerque was not sorry to go to the rescue of the Portuguese prisoners. He would have postponed this duty in order to obey the king's express commands; but now that the winds forbade him to sail East, he determined to sail West. He started with eighteen ships, carrying 1400 men; and though he lost one galley at sea, he arrived safely at the port of Pedir in the island of Sumatra in May 1511 with the rest of his fleet. At that place he found nine of the Portuguese prisoners, who had escaped from Malacca, and he then made his way slowly to the great city, which was said to contain a population of over 100,000 inhabitants.

For weeks negotiations went on with the Sultan of Malacca. The main point at issue was the surrender of Ruy de Araujo and his fellow-prisoners. Albuquerque declared he would make no treaty with the Sultan until the prisoners were delivered, and the Sultan on his part was resolved not to give them up until a treaty of peace had been signed. Under these circumstances Albuquerque wrote to the Factor, telling him that he and his companions must bear their hardships with patience. Ruy de Araujo replied in terms which show the gallant spirit of the Portuguese at that period.

> 'God grant,' he said, 'that neither the fleet of the King of Portugal, nor his Portuguese should receive any affront or discomfiture in order to make his life secure, for he was also on his part bound to die for the service of God and his King, and for the liberty of his countrymen, and he held it to be a good fortune for him that Our Lord had placed him in a state where he could die for his Holy Faith; and as for himself and his companions, he should not fail to do what was best for the service of the King of Portugal, for they were now quite resigned to anything that could happen to them; and he would have Affonso de Albuquerque to know that the King of Malacca was making ready as fast as was possible, and that it was the Gujarátís who were at work day and night upon the fortification of the stockades, for these were the principal people who could not bear that the Portuguese should get a footing in the land; and if the Portuguese attack upon the city should be decided upon, it ought to be put into execution as quickly as could be, without wasting any more time in discussing terms of agreement or making demands for the surrender of the Christians; for he must know for certain that the King would not restore them except under compulsion; and he was now become so puffed up with pride when he surveyed the great number of foreign soldiers that he had, that he thought of nothing less than actually capturing the Portuguese fleet.'[27]

Acting on the unselfish advice given to him, Albuquerque sent some boats to set fire to the ships in harbour and the water-side houses. The Sultan immediately gave in, and sent Ruy de Araujo and his companions safely on board the Portuguese fleet. Negotiations still continued, and Albuquerque became convinced at last that the Sultan was endeavouring to delay him until the change of the monsoon should make it impossible for him to return to India that season. He therefore resolved to attack Malacca at once. Ruy de Araujo informed him that the key of the city was a certain bridge which united its two portions. The Governor divided

[27] Albuquerque's *Commentaries,* vol. iii. pp. 92, 93.

his forces into two battalions, which were to attack the bridge from either extremity; and he fixed the day of his patron Saint, St. James the Greater, July 25, for the assault.

One division was led by Dom João de Lima, Gaspar de Paiva, and Fernão Peres de Andrade; the other by Albuquerque himself and Duarte da Silva. Each did what was required, and the bridge was carried. The Governor then gave orders to build stockades on each side of the bridge, in order that they might spend the night there; but the men became wearied by the constant attacks made upon their position, and towards the evening the Portuguese set fire to the city and returned to their ships. Special mention is made of the use of elephants during this action, but the animals were wounded and did more harm to the Malays than to the Portuguese.

The withdrawal of his tired-out soldiers did not dishearten Albuquerque, and he resolved to call a council of his captains to obtain their consent to renewing the attack with the idea of permanently occupying the city, and building a fortress there; for he had experienced both at Ormuz and at Goa the great distaste entertained by the Portuguese captains for the work of building fortresses. The policy of Almeida, who preferred factories to fortresses, had always plenty of adherents who could not appreciate the imperial notions of Albuquerque.

A report is given of the speech which Albuquerque is said to have delivered to his captains, both in Correa and in the *Commentaries*. It is not probable that he actually spoke these words, any more than the Roman generals in Livy made use of the very sentences attributed to them. But the language is thoroughly consonant with Albuquerque's character, and exhibits the aims of his policy so clearly that the oration deserves quotation. The text here selected is that of the *Commentaries,* which is fuller than that given by Correa.

> 'Sirs,' he is reported to have said, 'you will have no difficulty in remembering that when we decided upon attacking this city, it was with the determination of building a fortress within it, for so it appeared to all to be necessary; and after having captured it, I was unwilling to let slip the possession of it, yet, because ye all advised me to do so, I left it and withdrew; but being now ready, as you see, to put my hands upon it again once more, I learned that you had already changed your opinion: now this cannot be because the Moors have destroyed the best part of us, but on account of my sins, which merit the failure of accomplishing this undertaking in the way that I had desired. And, inasmuch as my will and determination is, so long as I am Governor of India, neither to fight nor to hazard men on land, except in those parts wherein I shall build a fortress to maintain them, as I have already told you before this, I desire you earnestly, of your goodness, although you all have already agreed upon what is to be done, to freely give me again your opinions in writing as to what I ought to do; for, inasmuch as I have to give an account of these matters, and a justification of my proceedings to the King Dom Ma-

noel, our Lord, I am unwilling to be left alone to bear the blame of them; and although there be many reasons which I could allege in favour of our taking this city and building a fortress therein to maintain possession of it, two only will I mention to you on this occasion as tending to point out wherefore you ought not to turn back from what you have agreed upon.

'The first is the great service which we shall perform to Our Lord in casting the Moors out of this country, and quenching the fire of this sect of Muhammad so that it may never burst out again hereafter; and I am so sanguine as to hope for this from our undertaking, that if we can only achieve the task before us, it will result in the Moors resigning India altogether to our rule, for the greater part of them—or perhaps all of them—live upon the trade of this country, and are become great and rich, and lords of extensive treasures. It is, too, well worthy of belief that as the King of Malacca, who has already once been discomfited and had proof of our strength, with no hope of obtaining any succour from any other quarter—sixteen days having already elapsed since this took place—makes no endeavour to negotiate with us for the security of his estate, Our Lord is blinding his judgment and hardening his heart, and desires the completion of this affair of Malacca: for when we were committing ourselves to the business of cruising in the Straits of the Red Sea, where the King of Portugal had often ordered me to go (for it was there that His Highness considered we could cut down the commerce which the Moors of Cairo, of Mecca, and of Jeddah carry on with these parts), Our Lord for His service thought right to lead us hither; for when Malacca is taken, the places on the Straits must be shut up, and they will never more be able to introduce their spices into those places.

'And the other reason is the additional service which we shall render to the King Dom Manoel in taking this city, because it is the headquarters of all the spices and drugs which the Moors carry every year hence to the Straits, without our being able to prevent them from so doing; but if we deprive them of this, their ancient market, there does not remain for them a single port nor a single situation so commodious in the whole of these parts, where they can carry on their trade in these things. For after we were in possession of the pepper of Malabar, never more did any reach Cairo, except that which the Moors carried thither from these parts, and the forty or fifty ships, which sail hence every year laden with all sorts of spices bound to Mecca, cannot be stopped without great expense and large fleets, which must necessarily cruise about continually in the offing of Cape Comorin; and the pepper of Malabar, of which they may hope to get some portion, because they have the King of Calicut on their side, is in our hands, under the eyes of the Governor of India, from whom the Moors cannot carry off so much with impunity as they hope to do; and I hold it as very certain that, if we take this trade of Malacca away out of their hands, Cairo and Mecca will be entirely ruined, and to Venice will no spices be conveyed, except what her merchants go and buy in Portugal.

'But if you are of opinion that, because Malacca is a large city and very populous, it will give us much trouble to maintain our possession of it, no such doubts as these ought to arise, for, when once the city is gained, all the rest of the kingdom is of so little account, that the King has not a single place left where he can rally his forces; and if you dread lest by taking the city we be involved in great expenses, and on account of the season of the year there be no place where our men and our fleet can be recruited, I trust in God's mercy that when Malacca is held in subjection to our dominion by a strong fortress, provided that the Kings of Portugal appoint thereto those who are well experienced as governors and managers of the revenues, the taxes of the land will pay all the expenses which may arise in the administration of the city; and if the merchants, who are wont to resort thither—accustomed as they are to live under the tyrannical yoke of the Malays—experience a taste of our just dealing, truthfulness, frankness and mildness, and come to know of the instructions of the King Dom Manoel, our Lord, wherein he commands that all his subjects in these parts be very well treated, I venture to affirm that they will all return and take up their abode in the city again, yea, and build the walls of their houses with gold; and all these matters which here I lay before you may be secured to us by this half-turn of the key, which is that we build a fortress in this city of Malacca and sustain it, and that this land be brought under the dominion of the Portuguese, and the King Dom Manoel be styled true King thereof, and therefore I desire you of your kindness to consider seriously the enterprise that we have in hand, and not to leave it to fall to the ground.'[28]

After having made use of some such arguments as these, Albuquerque ordered a second attack on the city of Malacca. His success was as complete as it had been on St. James' Day, but the Portuguese on this occasion, instead of evacuating the place, at once commenced to build a fortress. The Sultan was driven out of the city, and was pursued into the interior by an army of 400 Portuguese and 600 Javanese.

The contingent of Javanese soldiers was obtained by an alliance which Albuquerque made as soon as he was in occupation of Malacca. When the Sultan fled, the Portuguese General ordered his men to spare the warehouses and other property of Ninachatu, the Hindu merchant who has been mentioned as the kind-

[28] Albuquerque's *Commentaries,* vol. iii. pp. 115-119.

ly benefactor of Ruy de Araujo and his companions in captivity. This leniency caused other Hindus to ask Albuquerque for his protection. He willingly granted it, and appointed Ninachatu as superintendent or governor of all the Hindus in the city. Then an aged Javanese, who had turned Muhammadan and was possessed of great wealth and influence, named Utemuta Rájá, also made his submission, and was appointed head of the Javanese community. He it was who supplied the Portuguese with the force of 600 Javanese soldiers.

Nor were these the only native trading communities which the Portuguese Governor favoured. He gave particular encouragement to the Chinese, the Burmese, who are generally called by the chroniclers Pegus, and the Loochewans; but he declared war to the death with the Malays, both as Muhammadans and as the former rulers. In spite of the assistance which the old Javanese chieftain had rendered him, Albuquerque was soon placed on his guard against the ambitious projects of Utemuta Rájá. Ruy de Araujo gave information that he was at the bottom of the plot formed in 1509 for the massacre of the Portuguese, and that it was his son who had sworn to assassinate Sequeira with his own hand. He further declared that if Albuquerque sailed away and left Utemuta Rájá in power, there would soon be an end of the Portuguese domination in Malacca.

Albuquerque gave heed to the warning, and when he found that the Javanese was taking advantage for his own profit of the power committed to him, he promptly had him and the principal members of his family arrested. They were tried before Pedro de Alpoem, the Ouvidor or Chief Magistrate of the Portuguese in the East, and condemned to death. The wife of Utemuta Rájá, who was a native of Java, promised to give a large sum of money in gold towards the expense of building the fortress, if the Portuguese would let her husband and children go. Albuquerque replied that the Portuguese did not sell justice for money, but that he was willing to hand over the corpses of the victims to be buried with native rites. The sentence was carried out in the great square of Malacca, where the treacherous banquet to Sequeira and his officers was to have been held, and Utemuta Rájá, his son, his son-in-law, and his grandson were all beheaded. The execution was followed by an attempted riot of the Javanese, which was easily suppressed.

This execution struck terror into the inhabitants of Malacca, and firmly established the Portuguese authority. Albuquerque then devoted himself, while the fortress was being constructed, to opening up relations with the neighbouring powers. He knew that the possession of Malacca would be of no advantage if traders were not encouraged to come to the city. It has been seen therefore that, while striking hard at the Malays, he gave every encouragement to the merchants of other nationalities. The most important of the trading nations, which brought their commodities to the Malay port, were the Chinese. Albuquerque had treated with great courtesy the crews of five Chinese junks, which were anchored in the harbour, at the time of the first assault on Malacca. After they had witnessed the valour of the Portuguese on that occasion, he allowed them to take in cargo and to depart in safety. These crews reported throughout China the bravery and civility of the Portuguese, which had a great effect upon the minds of the Chinese ministers; so much so, that when the expelled Sultan of Malacca appealed to China for help, and abused the Portuguese as robbers and pirates, he received the answer that the Portuguese seemed to be a very good people, and that the Chinese government would not assist him. Albuquerque did not at this time send an ambassador to China, but it is worthy of notice that it was one of his captains, Fernão Peres de Andrade, who, in 1517, was the first Portuguese to visit Canton.

With the kingdom of Siam Albuquerque himself opened up direct relations. When the five Chinese junks left Malacca, they took with them, at the Governor's request, Duarte Fernandes, who had learnt the Malay language while a prisoner with Ruy de Araujo, as an emissary to the Siamese Court. He was received most favourably by the King of Siam, who had always considered the Sultan of Malacca as an intruder and had heard the news of his defeat with joy. Fernandes returned to Malacca laden with rich presents, and Albuquerque sent him back to Siam, accompanied by a Portuguese fidalgo or gentleman, Antonio de Miranda, as ambassador. He also sent in different directions Duarte Coelho to visit Cochin China and Tongking, and Ruy da Cunha to the kingdom of Pegu. He entered into communications with the King of Java and with some of the chiefs of the island of Sumatra, who were all greatly impressed by the speedy conquest of Malacca.

Of equal importance was Albuquerque's despatch of three ships, under the command of Antonio de Abreu, to explore the Moluccas and the Spice Islands. This squadron was ordered not to take prizes, but to devote itself entirely to the work of exploration. It touched at many places, and did much important work, but its chief interest to later generations is that Francisco Serrão, who commanded one of the ships, carried with him a young Portuguese gentleman, Fernão de Magalhães, who was afterwards to make the first voyage round the globe in the service of Spain, and who, as Magellan, has left his name upon the map of the world.

In January, 1512, Albuquerque, after having completed his fortress, sailed from Malacca. He left an efficient garrison of 400 Portuguese soldiers, and placed the settlement under the governorship of Ruy de Brito Patalim, as Captain of the fortress, with Fernão Peres de Andrade under him as Chief Captain of the sea. Ruy de Araujo was re-appointed Factor, and also judge of suits between merchants of different nationalities. For each nationality in itself he appointed separate governors, of whom one was the faithful Hindu, Ninachatu. On his way back to India the famous ship *Flor de la Mar,* on which Albuquerque sailed, and which had been commanded during the Ormuz campaign by João da Nova, ran ashore on the coast of Sumatra, and since it was very old and rotten it broke up. Albuquerque and the crew were saved. But their dangers were not yet over, and the whole fleet would have perished from want of water and of supplies had they not met with and captured two Muhammadan ships.

When the Governor arrived at Cochin, there was great excitement, for, since no news had been received from Malacca, some of the officers had written to King Emmanuel that Albuquerque was lost with all his fleet. His first question, after returning thanks to Heaven in the principal church, was about the situation of Goa, his favourite conquest, and he was informed that it had been besieged throughout the winter, and was almost at the point of surrender.

The facts were that as soon as Albuquerque, the terrible governor, was known to be out of India, all his enemies, both native princes and reluctant captains, breathed more freely. The minister of the young King of Bijápur at once sent an army against Goa, under the command of Fulad Khán, whom the Portuguese called Pulatecão. This general defeated the forces of Timoja and Malhár Ráo, and then invaded the island of Goa, and established himself in the fortress of Benastarim. Timoja and Malhár Ráo fled to the court of the Rájá of Vijayanagar, where Timoja was poisoned, and Malhár Ráo soon after made his way to Honáwar, where he succeeded his brother as Rájá. The Portuguese garrison of Goa, under the command of Rodrigo Rebello, the Captain, marched out to attack Fulad Khán. But they had underrated the strength of their opponents. They were defeated, and among the slain were Rebello himself and the young Manoel da Cunha, son of Tristão da Cunha, whom Albuquerque had knighted for his gallantry at the capture of Goa.

According to Albuquerque's express commands, Francisco Pantoja should have succeeded to the governorship of Goa, but the captains resolved to pass him over, and elected instead Diogo Mendes de Vasconcellos. The new governor at once ordered Manoel de Lacerda to abandon the blockade of Calicut, on which he was engaged, and to come to the assistance of the besieged inhabitants of Goa. Diogo Mendes soon proved his unfitness for supreme command. The Court of Bijápur sent its most famous general, Rasúl Khán, with a strong army to the coast, but Fulad Khán refused to acknowledge his supremacy. Rasúl Khán then appealed for the help of the Portuguese against the insubordinate officer, and Diogo Mendes was foolish enough to comply. With the help of the Portuguese themselves, Rasúl Khán drove Fulad Khán out of Benastarim, and, once safely within the island of Goa, he demanded the surrender of the city.

This was too much even for Diogo Mendes, who now showed himself to be a brave commander. The city held out during the winter, but the inhabitants were much reduced by famine, and their power of defence was injured by the fall of part of the new wall, owing to the severity of the winter. Albuquerque, on hearing of the situation of affairs, sent a warrant for Manoel de Lacerda to be Captain of the city, and promised to arrive soon and destroy the besiegers. This news was received, in the words of the *Commentaries,* 'with a great ringing of bells and firing of salutes, for every one looked upon himself as redeemed from death.'[29]

But eagerly as Albuquerque desired to bring help to Goa, he sadly felt how inadequate were the forces that remained to him. The conquest of Malacca, and the necessity for leaving a garrison there, had much reduced his fighting strength, and he found that the officers he had left behind at Cochin were unwilling to lend him their aid. In fact, the agents or factors at Cochin, Quilon, and Cannanore looked with alarm at the establishment of the Portuguese in Goa. Their fears were shared by the native Rájás, who expected that the whole trade of the coast would be attracted from their ports to the new settlement. So strongly had this been felt, that the factors and their party, headed by Lourenço Moreno, the Factor at Cochin, had sent a despatch to King Emmanuel, during the period when they hoped the Governor had been lost in his expedition to Malacca, strongly advising the immediate

[29] Albuquerque's *Commentaries,* vol. iii. p. 206.

abandonment of Goa.

An effort was made to dissuade Albuquerque by Diogo Correa, Captain of Cannanore, who reported that an Egyptian fleet had set sail from the Red Sea for India, and advised Albuquerque to go against it, and not to the relief of Goa. After passing some weeks in a state of forced inactivity, Albuquerque, to his great joy, was reinforced by his nephew, Dom Garcia de Noronha, with six ships, on Aug. 20, 1512, and directly afterwards by a further squadron of eight more ships under Jorge de Mello Pereira. Both these captains brought with them a large number of soldiers. They also carried many young and gallant officers, who greatly distinguished themselves in the ensuing campaigns, among whom Dom Garcia de Noronha held the royal commission as Captain of the Indian Seas. The arrival of this young nobleman rejoiced the heart of Albuquerque, for it gave him a brave and faithful adherent, who almost replaced the loss he had suffered by the death of Dom Antonio de Noronha.

On September 10, 1512, Albuquerque set sail from Cochin with fourteen ships carrying 1700 Portuguese soldiers. He heard on his way that the report of the departure of an Egyptian fleet was unfounded; and he at once entered the harbour of Goa. He never doubted of victory, and instead of endeavouring to drive Rasúl Khán out of Benastarim, he resolved to blockade him, with his 6000 Turkish and Persian soldiers, in the castle there. For this purpose he sent Ayres da Silva to cut off the communications of the castle with the mainland. That captain, with six small ships manned by picked sailors, forced his way up the river, and after pulling up the stakes which the Muhammadans had fixed in the stream for their defence, he bombarded the castle under the eye of Albuquerque himself.

This operation cut off the retreat of the Muhammadan garrison, and Albuquerque made his entry into Goa. It is mentioned as characteristic of his extreme piety that he ordered the canopy of brocade which the chief men of the city were carrying over his head, to be borne instead over the Cross, which the priests had brought from their church to greet him. He then organised his military forces, and hearing that Rasúl Khán had marched out towards the city at the head of 3000 men, he resolved on fighting a pitched battle. He divided his infantry into three divisions, commanded respectively by Pedro Mascarenhas, Dom Garcia de Noronha, and himself; and he placed his cavalry, amounting to about thirty troopers, under Manoel de Lacerda. Owing to the Portuguese general's skilful dispositions the Musalmans were attacked simultaneously, in front by Mascarenhas and on the two flanks by the other divisions. The battle was very fierce, and the Muhammadans were driven into the castle of Benastarim.

The Portuguese endeavoured to follow them, and some of their leaders climbed upon the walls. The first who got up was Pedro Mascarenhas, and the author of the *Commentaries* states that,

> 'Affonso de Albuquerque after the rally embraced and kissed him on the face, whereat some were scandalised, although they had no need to be, for besides his actions that day like a brave cavalier, Albuquerque was under an obligation to him, for he had

> left the fortress of Cochin, of which he was Captain, and had come to serve the King in that war.'[30]

In spite of this gallantry it proved impossible to capture the castle by escalade, and Albuquerque ordered a retreat to Goa. Many officers and men were wounded in this engagement, and Albuquerque then determined to breach the fortress and carry it by storm. The trenches were pushed forward with much rapidity and an adequate breach was made, but on the very morning for which Albuquerque had ordered the assault, Rasúl Khán hung out the white flag. The terms which Albuquerque demanded were that the castle should be surrendered with all its artillery, ammunition and horses, and that the deserters in Rasúl Khán's camp should be given up to him. The Muhammadan general consented, but only on condition that the lives of the deserters should be spared. Benastarim was accordingly evacuated, and the island of Goa was once more left entirely in the hands of the Portuguese. The conquest had been made only just in time, for Rasúl Khán, as he retired with his disarmed troops, met a strong reinforcement coming up from Bijápur under the command of Yusaf-ul-Araj, whom the Portuguese called Içufularij.

This brilliant victory was marred by Albuquerque's cruelty to the Portuguese deserters who fell into his hands. Some of these men had gone over to the Muhammadan camp when the Portuguese ships were blockaded in the harbour of Goa in 1510, and the others had left Goa during the recent siege. Having promised to spare their lives, Albuquerque kept his word, but he mutilated them horribly, cutting off their ears, noses, right hands, and the thumbs of their left hands, and plucking out all their hair. The most conspicuous renegade, a fidalgo named Fernão Lopes, was also put on board a ship bound for Portugal in custody. He escaped, while the ship was watering at the island of St. Helena, and led a Robinson Crusoe life there many years.

The relief of Goa in 1512 completes the second period of Albuquerque's governorship. His tenacity in maintaining the Portuguese position at Goa is not less noteworthy than the valour by which he conquered it.

[30] Albuquerque's *Commentaries,* vol. iii. pp. 226, 227.

CHAPTER V

THE RULE OF ALBUQUERQUE (CONTINUED): THE EXPEDITION TO THE RED SEA AND CONQUEST OF ORMUZ

The conquest of Goa is so distinctly the most important event of Albuquerque's governorship, that it is expedient to make clear his aims and hopes with regard to the establishment of the Portuguese capital there. Fortunately a state paper is extant which defines the great Governor's position in eloquent words. When Dom Garcia de Noronha arrived at Cochin, he delivered to his uncle a letter from King Emmanuel directing that a general council of all the captains and chief officers in India should be held to consider the advisability of retaining Goa. The abandonment of the place had been recommended by four civilians, of whom the chief was, as has been said, the Factor at Cochin, with arguments that show how deeply the rival policy of the first Viceroy, Almeida, had taken hold of the Portuguese officials in India. They advocated the claims of commerce, as against empire, in language which vividly recalls that used by the English East India Company two centuries and a half later. The opinion of these opponents of Albuquerque was supported, at the Court of Lisbon, by Duarte de Lemos and Gonçalo de Sequeira, who had declined to share in the perils of the conquest.

The King embodied the ideas of the opposition in certain articles, which he sent to Albuquerque to submit to the consideration of his general council. These articles were: (1) that Goa was very unhealthy and was the cause of unnecessary expense, being of no use except to give trouble to the soldiers; (2) that therein there must always be continual war, for the King of Bijápur was so powerful, that he would be sure to try his utmost to recover it, because it was the chief port of his dominions; (3) that the revenues of the island, upon which Albuquerque laid great importance, could not be collected, except by maintaining a great number of people with heavy expenses for the collection of these revenues, since the King of Bijápur himself could not collect them without the assistance of a large army; (4) that the King of Bijápur would be glad to agree to any proposal, and to become tributary to His Highness the King of Portugal, provided that Goa was restored to him.

These articles were laid before the captains, who unanimously condemned them and stated—

> 'That they were amazed at His Highness desiring to surrender, in pursuance of the advice of men who had never donned a

> suit of armour for the sake of experiencing the trouble it would involve, a place so commodious and important as Goa, which had been acquired at the cost of so much Portuguese blood.'[31]

It may be doubted whether the council would have come to this decision had Albuquerque laid the subject before it before the relief of Goa, but he carefully left the point undecided, until after his great victory over Rasúl Khán and the capture of Benastarim.

Albuquerque's despatch upon the retention of Goa reveals the whole of his policy, and it must be carefully studied by anyone who wishes to understand the greatness of his views.

> 'Sire,' he wrote to the King, 'I captured Goa, because Your Highness ordered me to do so, and the Marshal had orders to take it in his instructions; I took it also, because it was the headquarters of the league which was set on foot in order to cast us out of India; and if the fleet which the Turks had prepared in Goa river (with a large force of men, artillery, and arms specially assembled for this object) had pushed forward, and the fleet from Egypt had come at this juncture, as they had expected, without doubt I should have been utterly discomfited; yea, even if ever so great a fleet had come from Portugal they would not have allowed it to make good its arrival in this country. But when once Goa was conquered, everything else was at our command without any further trouble, and when Goa was taken, that one victory alone did more for the advancement of Your Highness's prestige than all the fleets which have come to India during the last fifteen years. And if Your Highness, in deference to the opinions of those who have written this advice to you, thinks it possible to secure your dominions in these parts by means of the fortresses of Cochin and Cannanore, it is impossible; for, if once Portugal should suffer a reverse at sea, your Indian possessions have not power to hold out a day longer than the kings of the land choose to suffer it; for, if one of our men takes anything by force from a native, immediately they raise the drawbridge and shut the gates of the fortress, and this causes Your Highness not to be Lord of the land, as of Goa, for in this territory the injury which is done to Moors or to Portuguese does not reach beyond the Captain of the fortress. Justice is yours, and yours the arm, yours the sword, and in the hand of your Captain-General reposes the punishment, and before him lies the remedy for the complaint of everyone; and if to-day there be any improvement in regard to the obedience shown by the natives of the land, it is plainly to be referred to the fact that the taking of Goa keeps India in repose and quiet; and the fact that the island has so frequently been attacked by the Turks, as those who wrote to Your Highness assert, and so valiantly defended by

[31] Albuquerque's *Commentaries,* vol. iii. p. 264.

the Portuguese, enhances the credit which the progress of affairs in these parts deserves. And I have so completely disheartened the members of the league against us, that the King of Gujarát, powerful prince as he is, lost no time in sending to me his ambassadors and restoring to me all the cavaliers and fidalgos, who were shipwrecked with Dom Affonso de Noronha, my nephew, on their voyage from Socotra, without my sending to ask this of him, and even offered me permission to build a fortress in Diu, a matter of such immense importance that even now I can hardly believe it; and I am now importuned by the Zamorin of Calicut, who desires to grant me a site to build a fortress in his city, and is willing to pay a yearly tribute to the Crown. All this is the result of our holding Goa, without my waging war upon any of these princes.

'And I hold it to be free from doubt, that if fortresses be built in Diu and Calicut (as I trust in Our Lord they will be), when once they have been well fortified, if a thousand of the Sultan's ships were to make their way to India, not one of these places could be brought again under his dominion. But if those of your Council understood Indian affairs as I do, they would not fail to be aware that Your Highness cannot be Lord over so extensive a territory as India by placing all your power and strength in your navy only (a policy at once doubtful and full of serious inconveniences); for this, and not to build fortresses, is the very thing which the Moors of these lands wish you to do, for they know well that a dominion founded on a navy alone cannot last, and they desire to live on their estates and property, and to carry their spices to the ancient and customary markets which they maintain, but they are unwilling to be subject to Your Highness, neither will they trade or be on friendly terms with you. And if they will not have any of these things, how is it likely that they will be pleased to see us establishing ourselves in this city of Goa, and strengthening its defences, and Your Highness Lord of so important a port and bar as this is, and not labour with all their might to hinder us from accomplishing our intentions? And if it seems a hard matter to those who have written about this to Your Highness that the recovery of Goa should have been so many times attempted, how much harder must it have been to gain the country from so powerful a sovereign as the King of Bijápur, Lord of so many armies, who is not likely to refrain from straining every nerve to recover the possession of it and striking a decisive blow at our prestige, if he could do so? And whenever any one of his captains shall come up against this city, are we to surrender it immediately without first of all measuring our forces against him? If this be so, Your Highness may as well leave India to the Moors, than seek to maintain your position therein with such extraordinary outlays and expenses on the navy, in ships as rotten as cork, only kept afloat by four pumps in each of them.

'As for the extraordinary expenses connected with the maintenance of Goa, of which these idle fellows write to Your Highness, the mere dross of India is so great, that, if the Portuguese possessions be properly farmed by your officers, the revenue from them alone would suffice to repay a great part of these expenses to which we are put, and if they say that the reason why I desire to keep possession of Goa is because it was I who took it, Your Lordship may rest assured that if I were a Portuguese of such a character as they are, I would be the first, if you ordered me to destroy it, to put the pick axe into the walls, and to fire the barrel of gunpowder under the Castle, if only for the pleasure of seeing the cards of the game of India shuffled for a new deal; but as long as I live, and while it remains my duty to send an account to Your Highness of Indian affairs, Goa must not be dismantled, for I would not that my enemies should exult in the contemplation of any serious disaster to this estate; and I must sustain it at my own cost, until they get their wishes, and another governor be sent to rule over it.

'If this that I say does not agree with the ideas of some of those who are half-hearted about this matter of Goa, Your Highness may know for certain that as yet there is a man who is governing it; and old and weak as I am, I will accept the government of this conquered territory at Your Highness's hands, if it may be permitted me to confer the lands of the Moors upon the cavaliers and fidalgos who have assisted me to gain them. But do not require of me every year an account of what I am doing as if I were a tax-gatherer, because four ill-mannered fellows, who sit at home like idols in their pagodas, have borne false witness against me; but honour me, and thank me, for I shall be happy to complete this enterprise, and spend what little I have upon it; and, in conclusion, all that I have to say is, that, if Your Highness either now or at any other time surrenders Goa to the Turks, then plainly Our Lord desires that the Portuguese dominion in India should come to an end; and, as for me, Your Highness may be sure that, so long as I am Governor, although I be put to much trouble, I shall not at any rate send you painted pictures of fictitious places, but rather kingdoms taken by force of arms from their masters and fortified by me in such a manner that they may give a good account of themselves to all time.

'This is my opinion concerning this question of Goa which Your Highness commanded me to discuss with my captains and officers.'[32]

[32] Albuquerque's *Commentaries,* vol. iii. pp. 258-263.

These arguments of Albuquerque were convincing, and King Emmanuel wrote to him, that for the future he should consider it necessary to retain Goa. But at the same time the frank language which the great Governor had used, was turned to his disadvantage by his numerous enemies at the Court of Lisbon. It was suggested to the King, who was very jealous of his authority in the distant parts of Asia, that Albuquerque threatened and desired to make himself an independent prince at Goa. He was attacked as extravagant in his expenses and grandiose in his views, just as Lord Wellesley was censured by the directors of the East India Company nearly 300 years later. And these views became so prevalent at Court, that King Emmanuel resolved to supersede Affonso de Albuquerque.

The news of his disgrace did not however reach India until some months later, and Albuquerque carried out two interesting and important campaigns, the one in the Red Sea in 1513 and the other at Ormuz in 1515. It was not until after the relief of Goa that Albuquerque was at last able to carry out his favourite scheme of entering the Red Sea, and attempting to close that route to Muhammadan commerce. This was one of the primary aims of his policy. The various circumstances which had delayed its execution from year to year have been noted; and it was a curious irony of fate that the only scheme in which Albuquerque failed was the establishment of the Portuguese power in the Red Sea. Other things which he regarded as subordinate, such as the conquests of Malacca and Ormuz, were accomplished, but he was never able to become master of Aden.

Before he set sail, he sent in January 1513, a squadron under Garcia de Sousa to cruise off Dábhol, the next most important port of the King of Bijápur to Goa; he despatched three ships with artillery and reinforcements to Malacca; and he ordered Dom Garcia de Noronha to blockade Calicut. He then set to work to complete the defensive fortifications of the island of Goa. The events of the preceding siege showed that it was not sufficient to build a wall round the city of Goa, but that the whole island must be adequately fortified. For this purpose he rebuilt and strengthened the fortress of Benastarim, and also constructed castles and military works at Panjim and Divarim, since these three places commanded the most practicable passages across the rivers into the island. He appointed commandants for these forts, but placed over them Pedro Mascarenhas as Captain of Goa.

Albuquerque next sent ambassadors to the principal native princes, who desired to enter into negotiations with him. To the King of Ahmadábád or Gujarát he sent Tristão de Gá with a demand for leave to build a fortress in the island of Diu. To Bijápur he sent Diogo Fernandes to treat for peace. To the Rájá of Vijayanagar he sent Gaspar Chanoca with a request that the Portuguese should be allowed to build a fortress at Baticala. He also had an interview with Rasúl Khán, and heard from him that there were serious dissensions at the Court of Bijápur between the Turks and the Persians, which had culminated in the murder of Kamal Khán, the chief minister, who was a Persian. Having thus placed everything in the most secure situation possible, he appointed his cousin Jorge de Albuquerque to be Captain of Cochin in the place of Pedro Mascarenhas, and ordered Dom Garcia de Noronha to break up the blockade of Calicut and to join him with his fleet.

On February 7, 1513, Albuquerque sailed out of Goa harbour for the Red Sea with twenty ships carrying 1700 Portuguese and 800 native soldiers, the latter of whom had been recruited on the Malabar coast. He had a favourable voyage, and on Good Friday, March 25, 1513, he cast anchor in the harbour of Aden. The importance of Aden at the entrance to the Red Sea was at that time very great, as the ships from India and the further East all stopped there before proceeding to Egypt. It was not only merchant vessels which followed that route, but the numerous ships which carried Moslem pilgrims to the birthplace and the tomb of Muhammad at Mecca and Medina.

Albuquerque's intention was to put a stop alike to the passage of traders and of pilgrims. The chief who ruled at Aden was practically independent, but owed some fealty to the Sultans of Egypt. He possessed a powerful army, and the walls of his city were well provided with artillery. Nevertheless Albuquerque determined to assault the place by escalade. The Portuguese were nearly successful, but their over impetuosity caused all the scaling ladders to be broken by the crowds of soldiers who tried to mount them at once. Only a small party managed to enter the town, and since they could not be supported owing to the breakdown of the ladders, they were almost entirely cut to pieces. Several officers were killed in this affair, amongst whom were Jorge da Silveira and Garcia de Sousa, who both distinguished themselves by their daring valour. Finding it impossible to breach the walls from the sea Albuquerque then set out to explore the coasts of Arabia and Abyssinia.

The latter, as a Christian empire, and the seat of that mythical monarch, Prester John, was a subject of great interest to the Christians of Europe. It has been said that John II of Portugal sent one of his equerries João Peres de Covilhão to Abyssinia, where he had become a person of influence and eventually died. Ambassadors had also been sent to that country by way of Melinda in Vasco da Gama's second voyage to the East, and had been favourably received by David, the then Emperor of Abyssinia.

The existence Of such a Christian empire interested most Europeans only on account of its religion, but Albuquerque looked on it from a political aspect. He hoped to make use of the Abyssinians to attack Egypt from the South and overthrow the Muhammadan dynasty reigning there. In case this could not be accomplished, he formed a scheme by which the waters of the Nile should be diverted, so as to run through Abyssinia to the Red Sea, and thus destroy the fertility of Egypt. He even went so far in pursuance of his idea as to request the King of Portugal to send him experienced miners from the island of Madeira, who were accustomed to dig through rocks. Another plan he formed was to send a detachment to Medina to carry off the body of Muhammad. But he felt his present voyage to be rather one of exploration, and so, after sailing about throughout the summer of 1513, he left the Red Sea in the month of August for India. This cruise was one of great importance to the Portuguese, and a knowledge of the coasts, and of the navigation of the Red Sea was obtained, which proved in after years to be very useful. Before departing Albuquerque burnt many of the ships which were moored in the harbour of Aden, and he promised to return speedily and conquer the city.

On leaving the coast of Arabia, Albuquerque sailed direct to Diu. The situation of affairs in Gujarát had somewhat altered. Mahmúd Sháh Begára had always been willing that the Portuguese should build a fortress there, and his willingness may be attributed to the fact that Málik Ayaz, the Nawáb of Diu, had become practically independent of him. This Muhammadan ruler had been the declared enemy of the Portuguese ever since the days of the first Viceroy, Dom Francisco de Almeida. He had assisted the Emir Husain in the naval battles of Chaul and Diu, and had formed a high idea of the power of the Portuguese. He now submitted to Muzaffar Sháh II, who had just succeeded as King of Gujarát, and implored him not to grant permission for the Christians to build a fortress at Diu. He consented however to the foundation of a factory, and Albuquerque accordingly left one ship behind him, when he sailed south, with Fernão Martins Evangelho as Factor. On their way to Goa the Portuguese seized all the Muhammadan ships which had that year left Calicut, and had not yet been able to get across the Indian Ocean because of the monsoon, which is said to have completed the ruin of the Mopla merchants of Calicut. Albuquerque also left a squadron under Lopo Vaz de Sam Paio to blockade the port of Dábhol, and he then returned safely to Goa.

The year 1514 is the most peaceful of Albuquerque's administration. In it he was occupied mainly with matters of internal policy and the strengthening of his relations with the native princes. The most important event of the year was the building of the fortress of Calicut, and though the policy by which he attained this end cannot be commended, the result was a remarkable conclusion to his transactions on the Malabar coast. The long and consistent opposition of the Muhammadans of Calicut to the establishment of the Portuguese power is one of the leading threads of the history of the period. From the time of Vasco da Gama's first voyage and the murder of the Portuguese factor in 1500, Calicut had been the headquarters of the enemies of Portugal. King Emmanuel never ceased reiterating his orders that Calicut should be conquered at any cost; he declared his honour to be involved in the destruction of the Zamorin's power; and the defeat and death of Dom Fernão de Coutinho exasperated him exceedingly.

By the fleet which was commanded by Dom Garcia de Noronha the most precise orders had been sent for the building of a fortress at Calicut, and Francisco Nogueira had brought out a royal commission to be Captain of it. The Zamorin, who had been much impressed by the conquest of Goa, now declared his willingness to grant a site for a fortress at Calicut, but he would not grant the only site which Albuquerque was inclined to accept, because it completely commanded the harbour. On his return from the Red Sea, Albuquerque was informed by Nogueira of the temporising policy of the Zamorin, and resolved to carry out the King's orders without more delay. He met with considerable opposition, especially from the Rájá of Cochin, who feared that the lucrative pepper trade, which he enjoyed, owing to the existence of a fortress and factory in his capital, would go to Calicut, and his views were adopted by the civil officers in charge of the trade and also by all the adherents of Almeida's policy. Nevertheless Albuquerque persisted, and since nothing could be done with the reigning Zamorin he advised the heir apparent to secure his accession by poison.

The advice was followed; the Zamorin was poisoned, and his murderer and successor allowed Albuquerque to build a fortress on the site he had chosen. It was the best fortified castle erected in India, and its water gate, by means of which reinforcements and ammunition could be introduced direct from the sea, was especially admired. The new Zamorin offered to pay full compensation to the Portuguese for all the damage that had been done since the murder of the first factor, and he also sent two native envoys to Lisbon to protest his sincere submission to King Emmanuel. The erection of the fortress at Calicut set the seal on the Portuguese power on the Malabar coast; the Mopla merchants were controlled at their headquarters, and the *Commentaries* assert that the Rájá of Narsingha or Vijayanagar

> 'declared, when he heard of it, that since the Zamorin of Calicut had assented to the building of a fortress in his land by the Portuguese, the Captain-General of India might as well build another in Bisnagar (Vijayanagar) if he pleased.'[33]

Though the building of the fortress at Calicut was the most important event of Albuquerque's rule in 1514, some notice must likewise be given to his relations with Gujarát, and the expeditions he sent to Ormuz and Malacca.

It was reported to him by the factor he had left at Diu, that the Nawáb of that place had gone to Ahmadábád in order to induce the King of Gujarát to refuse the Portuguese leave to build upon the island, and also that Ismáil Sháh, of Persia, had sent a special embassy to Ahmadábád to induce the King to accept the Shiah form of the Muhammadan religion. Albuquerque, on this, determined to send a better equipped embassy than before to the Court of Muzaffar Sháh II. He selected two fidalgos, on whom he could rely, Diogo Fernandes de Beja, who had been his flag captain in the Red Sea, and Jaymé Teixeira. The ambassadors arrived safely at Surat, but it was not until after a long delay that they were forwarded to Ahmadábád. They at once demanded of the Minister that the Portuguese should be allowed to build at Diu, and were told in reply that the very name of a fortress was distasteful to the King. The ambassadors replied

> 'that the King of Portugal's men and property could only be safe in a very strongly fortified fortress, so that it should not be exposed to robbery, nor the men to slaughter, things which it was notorious had been perpetrated in Calicut, Quilon, and Malacca.'[34]

The King then sent an answer that, as a favour to Albuquerque, he would grant a site for a fortress at Broach, Surat, Máhim, Dumbes, or Bukkur, but not at Diu. This offer was refused, and the King then asked whether the Portuguese would allow his ships to make their voyages in security to Aden, if they did not carry spices. Diogo Fernandes replied that this could not be allowed, and that the Gujarátís should be content with trading to Malacca, Burma, Bengal and Persia, which were allied to the King of Portugal, without seeking to go to Arabia where he was at war. After these questions had been discussed at length, the Portuguese ambassadors returned to Goa, and it was not till some years later, during the gov-

[33] Albuquerque's *Commentaries,* vol. iv. pp. 74, 75.

[34] Albuquerque's *Commentaries,* vol. iv. p. 101.

ernorship of Nuno da Cunha, that leave to build a fortress in Diu was granted to the Portuguese. Albuquerque was much pleased with the prudence and good behaviour of his envoys, which contrasted favourably with the outrageous conduct of the ambassador of Ismáil Sháh. It may be added that the King of Ahmadábád declined to accept the suggestion that he should become a Shiah.

From Malacca very bad news reached Albuquerque. Though the King of Siam and other neighbouring rulers had been kindly disposed to the Portuguese residents there, an energetic attack on their position was made by a fleet and army of Javanese, commanded by a former servant of Utemuta Rájá. The Captain of the fortress and the Captain of the fleet, who had been left in command, Ruy de Brito and Fernão Peres de Andrade, quarrelled, and their dissensions had nearly ruined the cause of the Portuguese. The latter had, however, won a considerable naval victory, and Albuquerque was inclined to favour him. He at once sent off three ships to Malacca, with whose help another great victory was won, and eventually he appointed his cousin, Jorge de Albuquerque, to be Captain of Malacca. This officer showed himself worthy of the confidence bestowed upon him; he defeated some insurgents who had risen against the King of Pacem, a native monarch in the island of Sumatra, which victory finally established the Portuguese influence in those quarters. Ruy de Brito returned to India, and under the government of Jorge de Albuquerque the Portuguese settlement in the Malay Peninsula remained in peace and tranquillity for some years.

A matter which occupied much of Albuquerque's attention was the establishment of the Portuguese power at Ormuz. He had never forgotten nor forgiven the slights which had been put upon him during the year 1508, and had long desired to complete the fortress which he had commenced, and carry out his vow of vengeance. The state of affairs in Persia increased his wish to act with promptitude. On his return from the Red Sea, he had been informed that the old King of Ormuz and his wily minister, Cogeatar (Khojah Atár), were dead, and what was of more significance, that the new king had acknowledged the supremacy and the form of religion of Ismáil Sháh. It was obvious that if the Portuguese did not strike quickly they would have to contend with the powerful Sháh of Persia for the possession of Ormuz. Albuquerque had found an ambassador from Ismáil waiting for him in India, to whom he exhibited the wealth and strength of the Portuguese establishments, before sending him back to Persia accompanied by an envoy from himself. It will be remembered that he had nominated Ruy Gomes as ambassador in 1510, and that that gentleman had been poisoned at Ormuz on the way. He now selected Miguel Ferreira for the office, with similar instructions to those given to Ruy Gomes. The Governor himself greatly impressed the Sháh's ambassador, and it is recorded

> 'That he was so struck with the personal appearance of Affonso de Albuquerque, that he desired a life-size portrait of him to be painted, which could be carried to Sháh Ismáil.'[35]

Ferreira was more fortunate than Ruy Gomes, and reached the Court of the Sháh of Persia in safety. He was received with the greatest honour; so much so

[35] Albuquerque's *Commentaries,* vol. iv. p. 81.

that the ambassador of the King of Bijápur was much offended that a better reception was given to the Portuguese emissary than to himself. Ismáil Sháh had many conversations with Ferreira, and declared 'the desire which he cherished for the destruction of the Grand Sultan and the house of Mecca.'[36] After the departure of his ambassador, Albuquerque sent the son of his cousin, Jorge de Albuquerque, a young man of much promise, named Pedro, in command of four ships, with instructions to visit Aden, to winter at Ormuz, and to explore the Persian Gulf. The young commander, on his arrival at Ormuz, found that the new King was entirely under the influence of a young Persian named Rais Ahmad, who had taken possession of Cogeatar's goods and endeavoured to occupy his position. Pedro de Albuquerque first demanded that the half-finished fortress commenced by the Governor should be handed over to the Portuguese. When excuses were made, he desisted from this demand owing to the weakness of his squadron, and contented himself with requesting that the tribute due to the King of Portugal for the last two years should be paid. He obtained 10,000 xerafins (under £750), and after exploring the Persian Gulf he returned to India. On hearing his report, Albuquerque resolved in the succeeding season to proceed himself to Ormuz.

On February 20, 1515, Albuquerque left Goa with twenty-six ships, after appointing Pedro Mascarenhas Captain of Cochin, and Dom João de Eça Captain of Goa. This was his last campaign, and it is interesting to notice that it took place in the same quarter as his first Asiatic enterprise. But Affonso de Albuquerque, the great Captain-General of India, the conqueror of Goa and Malacca, was a very different person to the Affonso de Albuquerque of seven years before, the commodore of a small squadron, holding an ambiguous position, and at issue with the Viceroy and his own captains. The terror of his name had now spread abroad, and his captains no longer dared to oppose his wishes. In the month of March he anchored off the island of Ormuz, and at once demanded that the half-finished fortress should be handed over to him. After much negotiating the King of Ormuz gave way, and the Portuguese landed to complete their fortress. But Albuquerque did not feel safe as long as Rais Ahmad preserved his influence at Court; he therefore had the young man assassinated before the King's eyes. This murder terrified the King, who then complied with all the wishes of the Portuguese.

Albuquerque's successive measures were taken with great skill; he first got the King to surrender all his artillery, on the ground that it was needed for the defence of the fortress against a fleet which was rumoured to be coming from Egypt; and he next persuaded the King to issue an edict that the inhabitants of Ormuz should be disarmed. The completion of the fortress occupied some months, at the close of which, in August 1515, Albuquerque unwillingly consented to the return of his favourite nephew, Dom Garcia de Noronha, to Portugal.

While at Ormuz he was visited by envoys from all the petty rulers along the Persian Gulf, and even by chiefs from the interior of Arabia, Persia, and Tartary. His accumulated labours by this period had broken down his health, but his fame was at its height.

---

[36] Albuquerque's *Commentaries,* vol. iv. p. 88.

> 'From all parts of the interior country so many were they who came daily into the fortress in order to look upon Affonso de Albuquerque that our people could not keep them back; and although his illness prevented him from going out very often, they begged those who were on guard at the doorway of the fortress to at least permit them to get sight of him, for they had come from their own country for this express purpose. And if at any time he rode on horseback, so large a crowd of people followed after him along the streets, that he could hardly make his way through them; and as the fame of his person, and his greatness, was the topic of all those parts, and in consequence of the news which the ambassadors whom Sháh Ismáil had sent to him had circulated, they sent their servants to him with orders to draw his portrait to the life.'[37]

Every day, however, the great Governor's health grew worse, and on September 26, 1515, he summoned all the captains to his residence in Ormuz, and declared to them that since his illness promised to prove fatal, he wished them to swear to obey whoever he nominated as his successor. On October 20 he appointed Pedro de Albuquerque Captain of Ormuz, and from that time gave up attending to business and began to prepare for death.

On November 8, 1515, he set sail from Ormuz in the *Flor da Rosa,* commanded by his faithful friend, Diogo Fernandes de Beja, hoping that he should end his days in Goa, the city which he had conquered and which he loved. But he was not allowed to conclude his great career without suffering a deep humiliation. On the way a native brigantine was captured, which contained letters directed to Albuquerque. In spite of his health he insisted on these letters being read to him at once. In them appeared the news that Lopo Soares de Albergaria had just reached India, with a commission to succeed him as Governor. This news wounded Albuquerque to the heart.

> 'He lifted up his hands and gave thanks unto Our Lord and cried:—"In bad repute with men because of the King, and in bad repute with the King because of the men, it were well that I were gone."'[38]

This harsh measure of supersession had undoubtedly been suggested to King Emmanuel by the personal enemies whom the Governor had made through his imperious temper; and it is not without significance that among the captains who accompanied Soares de Albergaria were two of Albuquerque's declared enemies, Francisco de Tavora and Diogo Mendes de Vasconcellos. The jealous disposition of the King had been freely worked on, and the argument that Albuquerque wished to make himself an independent prince or duke at Goa had had its effect. On receiving the tidings of his disgrace Albuquerque added a codicil to his will, directing that his bones should be carried to Portugal, and he wrote the following proud and touching letter to King Emmanuel, the sovereign he had served so well.

[37] Albuquerque's *Commentaries,* vol. iv. p. 181.
[38] Albuquerque's *Commentaries,* vol. iv. p. 195.

> 'Sire, I am not writing to Your Highness with my own hand, because, when I do so, I tremble very greatly, which is a warning of my approaching death. I leave a son, Sire, to perpetuate my memory, to whom I bequeath all my property, which is little enough, but I bequeath him also the obligation, due to me for all my services, which is very great. The affairs of India speak for me and for themselves [*lit.* for it]. I leave India, with its principal heads fallen, in your power, without its promising any other trouble, except the locking close of the gate of the Straits [*i.e.* of the Red Sea]; that is what Your Highness ordered me to do. I give you as my constant counsel, Sire, for the security of India, to continue drawing your expenses from it [*i.e.* to make the administration pay for itself]. I beg Your Highness in reward to remember all this, and to make my son a nobleman and to give him full satisfaction for my services. All my hopes I place in the hands of Your Highness and of the Queen. I commend myself to you both that you may make my affairs *[cousas]* great, since I make my end in the affairs of your service and for them deserve to be rewarded. And as for my pensions, which I have won for the greater part, as Your Highness knows, I kiss your hands for them for my son. Written at sea on the sixth day of December, 1515.'
>
> *In Albuquerque's own handwriting:—*
>
> 'Done by the servant of Your Highness,
> 'AFONSO D ALBOQUERQUE.'[39]

It is satisfactory to know that the King complied with the dying wish of the great Governor. Albuquerque's illegitimate son, Braz de Albuquerque, was recognised at Court and married to a rich heiress, Dona Maria de Noronha, daughter of the first Count of Linhares; he was granted a pension of 300,000 reis (about £66) a year; and his name was changed by royal command to Affonso. He proved himself worthy of his father, became Controller of the Household of King John III, and President of the Senate of Lisbon, but posterity is chiefly grateful to him for having compiled the *Commentaries* of his great father's deeds. King Emmanuel quickly regretted his unworthy treatment of his faithful servant, and in 1516, before the news of his death had reached Lisbon, he sent out orders that while Lopo Soares de Albergaria was to be Governor of Calicut, Cochin and Malacca, Albuquerque was to command in the Indian and Arabian Seas, with power to draw on all the resources of India for a final campaign in the Red Sea. This news, however, never reached the great captain, and the commission was not signed until after his death.

The details of the death of Affonso de Albuquerque are best told in the brief words of the *Commentaries*.

> 'At this time he had become so weak that he could not stand, ever desiring Our Lord to take him to Goa, and there do with

[39] This letter is translated from the original text preserved in the Torre del Tombo, or Archives of Portugal, printed in the *Cartas de Albuquerque,* vol. i. pp. 380, 381. The version given in the *Commentaries,* vol. iv. pp. 195, 196 is much shortened.

him as should be best for His service; and when the ship was yet distant three or four leagues from the bar, he ordered them to summon Frei Domingos, the Vicar-General, and Master Affonso, the physician. And as he was so weak that he could not eat anything, he ordered his attendants to give him a little of the red wine which had been sent that year from Portugal. And when the brigantine had sailed away in advance to Goa, the vessel proceeded to cast anchor on the bar, on Saturday night, the fifteenth day of the month of December. When they told Affonso de Albuquerque that he was at the end of his voyage, he lifted up his hands and gave many thanks to Our Lord, because he had vouchsafed to grant him that mercy which he had so earnestly desired, and thus he remained all through that night with the Vicar-General, who had already come off from the shore to the ship, and with Pedro de Alpoem, Secretary of India, whom he constituted his executor, embracing the crucifix and continually talking; and he desired the Vicar-General, who was his confessor, to recite the Passion of Our Lord, written by St. John, to which he was always devoted, for in it, and in that cross which was made in the likeness of that whereon Our Lord had suffered, and on His wounds he rested all the hope of his salvation; and he commanded them to attire him in the costume of the Order of Santiago, whereof he was a Commander, that he might die in it; and on the Sunday, one hour before the dawn, he rendered up his soul to God; and there finished all his troubles without seeing any satisfaction of them.'[40]

The corpse of the great governor was at once conveyed to Goa and

'so great was the crying and weeping on all sides, that it seemed as if the very river of Goa was being poured out.'[41]

The body was conveyed to the Chapel of Our Lady of the Conception, which he had founded outside the gates of Goa on the spot where he had witnessed the second capture of the city.

'There accompanied the procession,' it is recorded in the *Commentaries,* 'all the people of the city, not only Christians, but Hindus and Moors [Muhammadans], who filled the streets, demonstrating by the profusion of their tears the great sorrow they felt at his death. As for the Hindus, when they beheld his body stretched upon the bier, with his long beard reaching down to his waist, and his eyes half open, they declared, after their heathen notions, that it could not be that he was dead, but that God had need of him for some war, and had therefore sent for him.'[42]

His son, according to the last wishes of the great captain, desired to remove the body of Affonso de Albuquerque to Portugal, but King Emmanuel would nev-

[40] Albuquerque's *Commentaries,* vol. iv. p. 196.
[41] Albuquerque's *Commentaries,* vol. iv. p. 198.
[42] Albuquerque's *Commentaries,* vol. iv. p. 198.

er consent, saying that as long as the bones of Affonso de Albuquerque were at Goa India was secure. John III held the same view, and it was not until 1566, more than fifty years after his death, that his remains were removed to Portugal by permission of Queen Catherine, who was then Regent in the name of the boy-king, Dom Sebastian. They were then solemnly interred in the Chapel of Our Lady of Grace at Lisbon, attached to the Augustinian monastery, where they still repose.

The deeds of Albuquerque form his fittest memorial, and in the next chapter an attempt will be made to examine his character as exhibited by his internal policy. Nevertheless it is interesting to quote here his son's description of his person and his character as given in the *Commentaries*.

> 'This great Captain was a man of middle stature, with a long face, fresh coloured, the nose somewhat large. He was a prudent man, and a Latin scholar, and spoke in elegant phrases; his conversation and writings showed his excellent education. He was of ready words, very authoritative in his commands, very circumspect in his dealings with the Moors, and greatly feared yet greatly loved by all, a quality rarely found united in one captain. He was very valiant and favoured by fortune. King Ferdinand said to Pedro Correa, when he was Portuguese ambassador at the Spanish Court, that it was a very astonishing thing, that King Emmanuel, his son-in-law, should have ordered Affonso de Albuquerque to return from India, seeing that he was so great a captain and so fortunate in his wars. He always gained the victory in his battles against the Moors, both at sea and on land, sometimes indeed being wounded, for the places where he was posted were never of the safest. He was very prompt in the performance of any undertaking when he had once determined upon it, and his name and his successes are so celebrated among all the kings and princes of Europe and Asia, that the Grand Turk, when conversing with Don Alvaro de Sande, captain of the Emperor Charles V, whom he held in captivity, concerning the state of India, laid his hand on his breast and said that Affonso de Albuquerque had been a very remarkable captain. He was a man of the strictest veracity, and so pure in the justice he administered that the Hindus and Moors after his death, whenever they received any affront from the Governors of India, used to go to Goa to his tomb and make offerings of choice flowers and of oil for his lamp, praying him to do them justice. He was very charitable to the poor, and settled many women in marriage in Goa. For he was of such a generous disposition that all the presents and gifts which the kings of India bestowed on him—and they were numerous and of great value—he divided among the captains and fidalgos who had assisted him in obtaining them. He was very honourable in his manner of life, and so careful over his language, that the greatest oath which he ever took when he was very much enraged was this: "I abhor the

life that I live." He died at the age of sixty-three years, having governed India for six years.'[43]

[43] Albuquerque's *Commentaries,* vol. iv. pp. 199, 200.

CHAPTER VI

THE RULE OF ALBUQUERQUE (CONTINUED): HIS INTERNAL POLICY

The relations of Portugal with Asia were in their origin, and throughout the reign of King Emmanuel, based on the desire to monopolise the commerce of the East with Europe. The idea of the universal conversion of the heathen to Christianity did not develop itself until the reign of King John III, Emmanuel's eldest son and successor. The idea of empire preceded that of proselytism, and was first enunciated by Albuquerque. The three conceptions are all closely united in the later history of the Portuguese in India, but they were evolved separately, had separate origins and distinct aims.

The establishment of direct commerce after the voyage of Vasco da Gama, led inevitably to the imperial notions of Albuquerque. The history of the Dutch and English power in the East followed the same lines, and the parallels which can be drawn are numerous and striking. But the idea of universal conversion to Christianity was a purely Portuguese and sixteenth-century idea. The Dutch and the English East India Companies discouraged Christian missionaries; the Portuguese, on the other hand, in the later days of their ascendancy, made their whole system of government subservient to the propagation of the Christian faith. It is not necessary here to draw deductions from this striking contrast. It is purely a matter of speculation whether this difference was due to religious causes or to the idiosyncrasies of the different nations; but the fact remains, and gives a peculiar interest to the history of the Portuguese in the East, as connected with the history of the extension of Christianity.

The voyage of Vasco da Gama, as well as the explorations of Prince Henry the Navigator, was dictated by commercial causes alone. Incidentally the Portuguese were interested in the discovery of native Christians on the Malabar coast and of a Christian Empire in Abyssinia. But it cannot be too strongly insisted upon that the primary aim of the Portuguese was commercial and not religious. The idea of empire was forced on the Portuguese by the opposition they met with in the establishment of their commerce. Vasco da Gama had no idea of conquering the cities he touched at on the Malabar coast; he merely wished to open up trade relations. Cabral, who followed him, gave evidence of his peaceful intentions by sending the first Portuguese factor, Correa, ashore at Calicut with only a few clerks. But the murder of Correa and the subsequent attacks on the Portuguese factories at Cochin and Quilon showed that peaceful trade could not possibly be established in the then condition of the Malabar coast. It was necessary to supplement factories by fortresses, and it is significant that the first fortress built was founded by Albuquerque during his first voyage to India.

Here Dom Francisco de Almeida wished to stop. He considered it enough if the Portuguese had a few fortresses to protect their factors, and commanded the sea to protect their trading ships. Albuquerque went a step further. He held it to be inadequate for the Portuguese to possess only fortresses, and argued that they must rule directly over the cities and islands which were the principal seats of trade. The history of the Dutch and English in the East shows exactly the same progression. The merchants of those countries originally desired only to establish trade. They next found it necessary to build fortresses to protect their factors or agents. And finally they found it necessary to build up, much against the will of their employers at home, the Dutch Empire in Java, Sumatra, and the Spice Islands, and the English Empire in India. The growth of the latter is traced in other volumes of this series, in which the progress of the English from traders to rulers is exhibited.

But the causes which led to the erection of the Dutch and English empires in Asia differ in one point from those which led to the establishment of the Portuguese power. The former originated in the necessity for breaking the Portuguese monopoly of Asiatic commerce; the latter in the necessity for overthrowing the Muhammadan monopoly. And it may be noted incidentally that the Portuguese had the more difficult task. They had to break the Muhammadan connection with the whole of the East, with Persia and the Spice Islands as well as with India. Their means were not so adequate as those of the English and the Dutch, for they had to make the difficult passage round the Cape of Good Hope with smaller ships, and their appliances for war were weaker than those of their successors.

Indeed, had not the Portuguese connection with Asia been carried out by the whole of the royal power of Portugal, it may be doubted whether it could ever have attained its full development. The Crown of Portugal kept the trade with the East in its own hands as a royal monopoly, and was able to despatch great fleets with armies, in some instances, of 1500 soldiers on board. Whereas the Dutch and English merchant adventurers were unable to act on such a large scale. The existence of the Royal monopoly may have, in the end, affected the Portuguese development in the East prejudicially, but in the commencement it was absolutely necessary, for the whole strength of the little kingdom was needed to bear the strain of the continual despatch of men to Asia.

It has already been said more than once that the Eastern trade with Europe was in the hands, until the commodities reached the Levant, of Muhammadan traders. These traders were chiefly of Arab origin, especially on the Malabar coast, but the Arab immigrants were supported in nearly every place by native converts to the religion of Islám. Such Moslem merchants did not try to establish direct rule in the cities in which they settled. It is an instructive tradition which makes the Rájá Perumal, who ruled over the whole Malabar coast, retire to Mecca after his conversion to Islám. The Arab traders on the Indian coasts did not resemble the Muhammadan invaders from the North-West. Conversion was not with them a main incentive; but, as the Muhammadan historians show, they took good care that native Muhammadan converts should not be prejudiced by their change of religion. The sort of *imperium in imperio* of the Arab or Mopla merchants in the Malabar cities is fully described in the Tohfut-ul-mujahideen, which shows how the Muhammadan communities were bound together and preserved their independence with regard to the Hindu sovereigns. Such a situation would have entirely agreed with the first notions of the Portuguese visitors to India. But the natural jealousy of the Muhammadan merchants would not permit a new trading community to spring up side by side with them.

King Emmanuel with great sagacity perceived the true meaning of the rivalry between the Portuguese and the Muhammadans in the East. He grasped the fact that he had not to deal with the merchants alone; he understood that the whole force of Egypt and the Turks would be arrayed against him. No division of trade could in those days be expected. He therefore resolved to cut off entirely the midway connection between the Levant and the chief markets of Asia. For this purpose he directed the building of a fortress in the island of Socotra; for this purpose he continually urged his commanders to seize Aden and close the Red Sea to commerce; for this purpose he was willing to receive ambassadors from the Hindu princes of India, but would hear of nothing but war against the Muhammadans. His captains carried out his instructions to the letter. The atrocious acts of cruelty committed by all of them against Muhammadans may have been in part due to religious animosity and to their Portuguese origin, but they were not discouraged by the Portuguese monarch, who was inspired more by his anxiety to destroy their trade than their faith.

The despatch of the Egyptian fleet, which was defeated by Almeida, was a proof that King Emmanuel's fears were justified. The internal wars of the principal Muhammadan rulers alone prevented that fleet from being followed at once by others still more formidable. Fortunately for the Portuguese, however, at this very period the Sultan Selim I of Constantinople was engaged in fierce war with the Mameluke Sultan of Egypt, and Ismáil Sháh of Persia was at open issue with both dynasties. But the necessity for closing the former trade routes would not have led to the ruin and slaughter of Muhammadans settled in India itself, had they not systematically opposed the Portuguese.

Albuquerque, after his first conquest of Goa and after that of Malacca, showed himself ready to treat the Moslems with clemency. In both instances that clemency was abused. The Muhammadans of Goa undoubtedly favoured the advancing army of Yusaf Adil Sháh; and the Muhammadans of Malacca began to plot against the Portuguese supremacy as soon as it was firmly established. It was for these reasons that he ordered the indiscriminate slaughter of the Muhammadans of Goa on his second conquest of that city, and that he directed the execution of Utemuta Rájá at Malacca. It was impossible that the two rival trading nationalities could co-exist; the one was inevitably led to destroy the other.

The first means devised for the overthrow of Muhammadan commerce was the system of licenses. Before Albuquerque's arrival the Portuguese arrogated to themselves the right of seizing any ship which did not carry a license granted by the Portuguese authorities. When this custom had been thoroughly established, it was followed by the complete prohibition of all licenses to trade with the Red Sea. Even when such a powerful ruler as the king of Gujarát asked permission to send ships to Aden, Albuquerque refused, and every vessel carrying merchandise in that direction was regarded as legitimate prey. The next step to closing the sea by means of the superiority of the Portuguese vessels was to build fortresses in spots commanding the trade routes. This was why Albuquerque laid such weight on the necessity of building a fortress at Ormuz, and of endeavouring to capture Aden.

So far the policy of King Emmanuel, of Almeida, and of Albuquerque agreed. But the latter advanced beyond the notions of his sovereign and his predecessor in his endeavour to found a Portuguese empire in the East. His system rested on four main bases. He desired to conquer certain important points for trading purposes, and to rule them directly; he desired to colonise the selected districts by encouraging mixed marriages with the native inhabitants; where he could not conquer or colonise he desired to build fortresses; and where this was impracticable he desired to induce the native monarchs to recognise the supremacy of the king of Portugal and to pay him tribute. It is not necessary to illustrate Albuquerque's policy on all these points at greater length than has already been done. His building of fortresses has been shown in the instances of Calicut, Malacca, and Ormuz; much has been said of his policy of conquest with regard to Goa; and his effort to induce native monarchs to become tributary has been related with regard to the King of Ormuz, the Zamorin of Calicut, and the Rájá of Cochin.

But Albuquerque's policy of colonisation is unique in the history of the Europeans in India; it has been far-reaching in its results, and has profoundly influenced the present condition of the Portuguese in India. His notion of an Eastern empire differed entirely from that taken in subsequent centuries by the English. He had no horror of mixed marriages, no dislike of half-castes. On the contrary, he did all in his power to create a race of half-caste Portuguese. When Goa was taken for the second time he tried to induce as many Portuguese as possible to marry native women, and especially the wives of the Muhammadans he had killed. He presided at these marriages himself, and gave dowries to couples married as he desired. The class he particularly encouraged were the artisans, who had been sent out from Portugal as ship-builders, rope-makers, and workmen in the arsenals and dockyards. He was also urgent in inducing his gunners to marry.

His aim in this policy was to form a population which should be at once loyal to Portugal and satisfied to remain in India for life. Officers indeed might expect to return to the fatherland, but Europeans of inferior ranks were too valuable to be allowed to escape. In all it is narrated that about 450 Portuguese were married to native women before he left Goa for Malacca. A quaint account of Albuquerque's colonising policy is given in the *Commentaries:*—

> 'Those who desired to marry were so numerous, that Affonso de Albuquerque could hardly grant their requests, for he did not give permission, except for men of proved character, to marry. But in order to favour this work, as it was entirely of his own idea, and also because they were men of good character and had de-

served by their good services that this privilege should be granted to them, he extended the permission to marry far beyond the powers which had been assigned by the King Emmanuel, for the women with whom they married were the daughters of the principal men of the land. And he granted this favour, among other reasons, in order that when the Hindus observed what he did for their daughters and nieces and sisters they might with better willingness turn Christians; and for this reason he would not suffer any of the women to be enslaved, but ordered that they should be all taken away from the masters who had possession of them; and he divided among the married ones the lands, houses, and cattle and everything else that there was, to give them a start in life; and if the women whom he thus gave in marriage asked for the houses which had been in possession of their fathers or their husbands, he ordered that these should be so given, and therein they found many jewels and gold pieces which had been hidden underground and abandoned when the city was captured.'[44]

This colonising policy was carried out by Albuquerque both for moral and political reasons, but it was not approved by all the other Portuguese officers in India. Some of the Catholic clergy objected, in spite of his making baptism a preliminary to marriage, and Diogo Mendes, when Captain of Goa, did all he could to discourage the married men. Albuquerque dwells at length on this subject in the long despatch which he wrote to the king on April 1st, 1512, after his return from Malacca.[45] It was one of his favourite schemes, and was well suited to the inclinations of the Portuguese people. Possibly no other nation is so willing to intermarry with alien races as the Portuguese. In Portugal itself there remain many traces in the physiognomy of the people of the intermarriage of the original stock with descendants of the Moors and even of the negro slaves, who were largely imported; in Brazil, an important division of the population is descended from mixed marriages between the Portuguese settlers and the aboriginal tribes; and in India the number of Portuguese half-castes forms a recognised section of the Christian population. These men and women resemble natives more than Europeans, and often appear to have only a very small amount of European blood.

But however desirous Albuquerque might be to create a body of Portuguese colonists and half-castes, he knew he could not establish a complete power in India by this means alone. The proportion of Europeans must inevitably be small, and some means had to be devised for governing the natives. This was one of the arguments employed by the school of Almeida for abandoning Goa. At Cochin, for instance, the Portuguese authority was only supreme within the limits of the fortress, and the task of governing the city was left to the Hindu Rájá. But the conquest of the island and city of Goa produced a new set of conditions, and for the first time a civilised European state had to provide for the government of Hindus. Albuquerque boldly faced the difficulty. He declared that the expenses of government must be met out of revenue, and that the ownership of Goa should not cause

[44] Albuquerque's *Commentaries,* vol. iii. pp. 41, 42.

[45] *Cartas de Albuquerque,* vol. i. pp. 29-65.

any drain on the king's finances. He did not at first design to administer the island by Portuguese officials, but resolved to farm out its revenues to native chiefs.

After the first capture of Goa, Albuquerque selected Timoja; after the second conquest, Malhár Ráo; and when the latter became Rájá of Honáwar, he received an offer for the situation from the Rájá of the neighbouring Hindu state of Vengápur. He was informed after the first conquest that the King of Bijápur had doubled the amount of the taxes levied by the Hindu Rájá of Vijayanagar. A petition was made that the latter amount should be exacted in future, and Albuquerque consented. Various sums are given as the value of these taxes, but perhaps the best and most trustworthy sum is 150,000 xerafins, a sum equivalent to about £9375. But at the same time, Albuquerque stated that if ever the payment of the taxes should fall into arrears the amount should be raised to that paid to Yusaf Adil Sháh.

The particular form of administration adopted by the first European rulers of an Indian District is of peculiar interest to Englishmen, who now administer nearly the whole of India. Unfortunately, the *Commentaries* give but a very few lines to this subject, and the contemporary Portuguese historians are practically silent. It will be as well therefore to give in full the description of the *Commentaries*.

> 'Timoja and the others received, in the name of the people, the lands, with these conditions that Affonso de Albuquerque laid down [*this refers to the reduction in the amount of the taxes*]; but it had also to be stipulated that he should appoint over them a Tanadar, and Hindus to govern them. Affonso de Albuquerque told them that he would promise not to appoint any Muhammadan to the office of Tanadar, and that he would give orders that the taxes should be collected by Portuguese in combination with certain Hindus of the land to be appointed by Timoja, in order that everything should be done with the least oppression of the people. And after having thus arranged the matter for them, Affonso de Albuquerque commanded that an oath should be administered to them, according to their heathen manner, that they would account for these taxes with him or the Governor of India for the time being; and he ordered that two pacharins should be given to each one, for it was an ancient custom in the land to give these to these Hindus.
>
> 'On the conclusion of this business, Affonso de Albuquerque gave them permission to return to their houses and to commence the collection of the taxes, according to the local registers of the lands. And they desired him to appoint over them certain Tanadars, who have the same office as our Almoxarifes [*Receivers of the Customs*], to collect the revenue and to dispense justice amongst them. In order to content them, Affonso de Albuquerque nominated Braz Vieira over them as Tanadar of Cintacora, and Gaspar Chanoca to act as his Secretary, and over all the other offices of Tanadar he appointed for them as Tanadars a number of honourable men, servants of the King, in whom he had complete confi-

> dence, to execute justice among them. And he ordered Timoja to appoint to each of these officers a Hindu clerk, in order to show them the method to be pursued in collecting the revenue; and to each Tanadar he told off 200 peons of the country to accompany them and carry out the instructions of their masters in the collection of the revenue. And he sent João Alvares de Caminha, who was a very honourable man and possessed great authority, in order to set those things in action as they should be carried on; and to put them into working order; and to repose in him a confidence with regard to other greater matters; and to be his clerk Antonio Fragoso was appointed; and a Hindu servant of Timoja to show him the register-books of the lands, how they were held in separate occupation, in order that there should be no dishonesty. And João Alvares de Caminha managed everything in such a manner that everybody was well pleased. The Hindus who had fled out of Goa returned to their original dwelling-places in the land immediately that they perceived that Affonso de Albuquerque had remitted to them a moiety of the dues, which they had been accustomed to pay to the Sabaio (Yusaf Adil Sháh), and had appointed natives over them to govern them.'[46]

It will be seen from the above quotation that the union of revenue and judicial functions, which is one of the principal features of the English administration of India, was adopted by Albuquerque in his settlement of Goa. So also was the co-operation of native with European officials, while João Alvares de Caminha was the first forerunner of the modern English Collectors of Districts. It will be observed that the native system of government was adopted, for mention is made of the land register which would contain the amount to be paid by each tenant in the form of rent. Albuquerque carefully maintained the constitution of the village communities, and shortly after his death, in 1526, a register called the *Foral de Usos e Costumes,* containing the peculiar usages and customs of the village communities, was compiled, which served as a guide-book to subsequent administrators. His use of Hindu clerks in the work of settlement is also noteworthy; he quickly perceived the adaptability of the natives, and desired to employ them not only in the collection of the revenue, but in the management of the Portuguese factories. To make this possible he understood the necessity of educating the future clerks in Western customs and languages. He established schools for the purpose, and in his famous despatch of April 1, 1512, he begged King Emmanuel to send out from Portugal a competent schoolmaster for the education of native clerks.[47]

Albuquerque likewise understood the value of native troops. In his expedition to the Red Sea he employed 800 native soldiers, who are stated to have been enlisted from among the inhabitants of 'Kánara and Malabar.' These men did good service, and were employed in other important expeditions. It is nowhere stated, however, whether they were drilled and commanded by European officers. The natives who served in the second capture of Goa were commanded by Malhár

[46] Albuquerque's *Commentaries,* vol. ii. pp. 125-127.

[47] *Cartas de Albuquerque,* vol. i. p. 43.

Ráo, and it seems most probable that the contingent in the Red Sea remained under their native officers.

In one thing only did Albuquerque venture to oppose the customs of the natives of India. He dared to prohibit in the island of Goa the practice of *Satí* or widow-burning, which was not abolished in British India until the governorship of Lord William Bentinck in 1829. The mention of Albuquerque's abolition of *Satí* in the *Commentaries* is sufficiently quaint to deserve quotation.

> 'They had a custom that if any Hindu died, the wife had to burn herself of her own free will; and when she was proceeding to this self-sacrifice it was with great merrymaking and blowing of music, saying that she desired to accompany her husband to the other world. But the wife who would not so burn herself was thrust out from among the others, and lived by gaining, by means of her body, support for the maintenance of the pagoda of which she was a votary. However, when Affonso de Albuquerque took the city of Goa, he forbad from that time forward, that any more women should be burned; and although to change one's customs is equal to death itself, nevertheless they were happy to save their lives, and spoke very highly of him because he had ordered that there should be no more burning.'[48]

Albuquerque, like Warren Hastings and other English governors-general, understood the importance of keeping his employer in a good temper by looking after his commercial interests. In all his despatches he always set forth the commercial advantages of his different conquests, and excused his imperial ideas by defending them on commercial grounds. Nothing more need be said here on the general question of the advantages and history of the direct trade route round the Cape of Good Hope, but some special instances of Albuquerque's sagacity in commercial matters deserve record. His establishment of a Portuguese factory at Malacca is a striking example of his sagacity. He perceived that though the pepper and ginger which was taken on board in the Malabar ports was grown in India, the cinnamon purchased there chiefly came from Ceylon, and the spices from the Malay Peninsula and the Spice Islands. He therefore took steps to open up a direct trade in cinnamon with Ceylon, and made his famous expedition to Malacca. By such measures he hoped to avoid having to pay the middleman's profits for conveying these commodities to India.

A smaller point also deserves notice. When the Portuguese factory was established at Cochin certain prices were fixed which had to be paid in gold to the Rájá's officers for the commodities required. This necessitated a considerable export of bullion from Portugal or else the forced sale of European goods. When Albuquerque was able to dictate terms to the new ruler of Calicut, he bargained that the products of India should be exchanged for merchandise brought from Portugal, and not sold for ready money. This reform was very unwelcome to the Portuguese factors and officials, who had hitherto made large profits by selling the European goods and embezzling part of the price paid for them.

[48] Albuquerque's *Commentaries,* vol. ii. p. 94.

One interesting proceeding of Albuquerque was his establishment of a new coinage, both at Goa and at Malacca. After the first capture of the future capital of Portuguese India, Timoja, whom he had made governor of the island, came with the principal inhabitants of the city and begged Albuquerque to strike some new money. The Governor replied, after holding a council of his captains, that he could not venture to assume one of the chief prerogatives of royalty without first obtaining the permission of the King of Portugal. But the need of a new currency was so urgent that Timoja and the inhabitants made a fresh petition that, if the Governor would not issue coins of his own, he would allow those of the King of Bijápur to pass current. This argument was irresistible, and Albuquerque established a mint for the coinage of gold, silver, and copper, under the superintendence of Tristão de Gá. The new money was inaugurated with an imposing ceremony. A proclamation was issued that the King of Bijápur's coins should not be kept or passed under severe penalties, and that whoever had any was to exchange it at the mint for the new coins. Albuquerque did not invent new measures of value; he adopted the Hindu values and simply gave Portuguese names to coins which he minted of the size and weight of those then in circulation in the country.[49] In Malacca however he appeared as an originator. The only coins used there were made of pewter or tin; there was no gold or silver coinage, and trade was carried on by barter. Gold and silver was brought into the Peninsula from China and Siam, but it was used as merchandise and not as money. Albuquerque altered this, and established for the first time a gold and silver currency. But he was too wise to neglect the original native money. The tin mines of the peninsula were made crown property, and tin and pewter coins were struck of the old values. The new currency was inaugurated at Malacca as it had been at Goa, with a grand ceremony, which is fully described in the *Commentaries,* in which it is quaintly remarked that the people especially approved of the distribution among themselves of the new coins, which were scattered by the Portuguese officials from the back of an elephant.

It is important to grasp the fact that Albuquerque did not commence the policy of wholesale conversions to Christianity. Franciscan friars accompanied him to India, as they had accompanied his predecessors, but their principal duty was to look after the spiritual welfare of the Portuguese and not to convert the natives. These friars included men of different types. Some were employed in political capacities, as for instance, Frei Luis, who was sent as ambassador to the Rájá of Vijayanagar. Some showed themselves men of the highest character, like Frei Francisco Loureiro, who was taken prisoner by the King of Gujarát on being wrecked on his coast with Dom Affonso de Noronha. The worthy priest was allowed to go to Cochin in order to procure a ransom for himself and his comrades in captivity. This occurred during Albuquerque's absence in Malacca, and the Portuguese officials at Cochin refused to furnish the money required. The friar at once returned to Gujarát to his imprisonment to the great admiration of the Muhammadan king. Some clerics, however, did not show themselves worthy of their profession. One in particular, a Dominican friar, embezzled the property of deceased Portuguese by

[49] A valuable monograph on the Portuguese coinage in India has been published under the title of *Contributions to the Study of Indo-Portuguese Numismatics,* by J. Gerson da Cunha, Bombay, 1880.

declaring that they had signed wills in his favour.[50] This man was promptly sent back to Portugal in disgrace.

But though the making of converts did not at once become the principal occupation of the Catholic clergy in India, some baptisms on a large scale took place after the capture of Goa. These were principally of the Muhammadan women, whose husbands had been slain, and whom Albuquerque gave in marriage to his favourites. His marriage scheme itself was severely condemned by some of the friars, and but for his own strong will might have caused a schism. But though he did not make missionary effort a main aim of his policy, like some of his successors, Albuquerque was unfeignedly pious. He built churches at Goa, at Malacca, and in the island of Socotra, and he granted in these instances the whole of the property which had belonged to the Muhammadan mosques to the new foundations. The first Portuguese adventurers in India were too delighted to find Christians at all in India to have time to examine into the difference of their ritual from their own. They were overjoyed to find a cross in digging foundations for a church in Goa. They believed that Christianity would quickly spread over the East. And the religious persecutions which mar the later history of the Portuguese in India were not thought of in the days of the great governor.

The causes of Albuquerque's triumphant progress in Asia may be found in a consideration of certain special and general reasons as well as in his own character.

The chief general cause was the weakness and mutual enmity of the rulers with whom he came in contact. He had not to strive with the great Mughals; he did not come directly in contact with Ismáil Sháh, who favoured instead of opposing him; nor did he have cause to attack the powerful Emperor of China. The Hindu Zamorin of Calicut, the Muhammadan Nawáb of Diu, the half savage Sultan of Malacca, the Arab King of Ormuz, were none of them great and powerful monarchs. All had external as well as internal enemies, and Albuquerque was quick to perceive and make use of this circumstance. The only great ruler he came into opposition with was Yusaf Adil Sháh of Bijápur, who, fortunately for the Portuguese, died in 1510. The division of India into hostile kingdoms was especially favourable to the progress of the Portuguese. Albuquerque was able to play off Hindu Rájás against Muhammadan kings: nor were monarchs even of the same faith necessarily united in bonds of friendship. Thus the Rájá of Cochin was the declared enemy of the Zamorin of Calicut, and the Muhammadan kings of the Deccan were too busy in fighting over the disruption of the great Báhmani kingdom to make a general effort against the new-comers. The existence of local jealousies and rivalries enabled Albuquerque, like later European rulers of India, to make good the position of his countrymen.

The special causes of the success of the Portuguese are to be found in the superiority of their ships, their artillery, and their soldiers. The Portuguese ships at the beginning of the sixteenth century, though much smaller than the great galleons which they afterwards built for the Indian trade, were much more efficient than the Arab vessels. They had to be both well built and well fitted to accomplish the long and perilous voyage round the Cape of Good Hope, whereas the Arab ships

[50] *Cartas de Albuquerque,* vol. i. p. 30.

were only intended to sail across the Indian Ocean with the favourable monsoon and then up the quiet waters of the Red Sea or Persian Gulf. But the Portuguese did not depend on sailing vessels alone in their maritime battles; they built galleys in imitation of the native craft, and secured good sailors for them by offering increased pay.

The excellence of the Portuguese artillery and the skill of the gunners was another main cause of their victories. The natives, indeed, understood the use of powder and of cannon; as many as 300 pieces of ordnance were captured at Malacca; but the Portuguese guns were always better served than those of their opponents. It was noticed at the siege of Benastarim that one of Rasúl Khán's guns did more damage than the rest, and it was soon discovered that it was being served by a Portuguese renegade. The arquebuses or clumsy muskets of the Portuguese also did them good service, though they cannot be compared to the more efficient arms of precision which came into use in the next century. Bows and arrows were the chief weapons on both sides, and the superiority of the Portuguese crossbowmen is constantly described in different engagements.

But neither ships nor arms would have effected much without brave hearts. And the Portuguese, in this their heroic period, gave evidence of a tried and adventurous courage which has seldom been equalled. Albuquerque's most serious repulse, at Aden, was due not to the reluctance but to the over impetuosity of his men. Again and again proofs of conspicuous gallantry were given, and many anecdotes might be quoted which testify to the bravery of both officers and men. But the discipline of the Portuguese was not equal to their courage. The soldiers and sailors were always ready to follow their officers, but the officers were apt to have ideas of their own with regard to the duty of obedience. The insubordination of Albuquerque's captains during his first expedition against Ormuz was imitated on many other occasions. Even the most severe examples failed to establish perfect discipline, and it was by no means the worst of the captains who were the most disobedient. But in spite of this defect the soldiers and the officers of Albuquerque were worthy of their leader. They had inherited their warlike disposition from their fathers; they had been trained to courage and endurance through centuries of fighting with the Moors both in the Peninsula and in Morocco; and their hideous cruelty to their conquered foes was as much a part of their nature as it was typical of the century in which they lived.

Albuquerque's own character counted for much in his success. He was comparatively an old man when he took up his governorship, and his scheme of policy was by that time carefully matured. To that policy he adhered unflinchingly from the beginning to the end of his career. His extraordinary tenacity of purpose was one of his most remarkable characteristics. He swore at the time of his first repulse at Ormuz that he would return, and he did. He insisted on the capture and retention of Goa, in spite of many varieties of opposition, and he gained his point. There can be little doubt that had he survived he would have succeeded in his cherished ambition of conquering Aden and closing the Red Sea to the commerce of the East.

With this tenacity of purpose went a wide and remarkable tolerance. The favourable countenance he showed to the Hindus was due to his nature as well as to his scheme of policy. With regard even to the Muhammadans, whom he hated, he could show a certain tolerance which would not have been found in a crusader. He sent embassies to Sháh Ismáil, and the Kings of Gujarát and Bijápur, and was ready to bear with the Moslems in Malacca and in India, until he grasped the irreconcilable nature of their enmity to the Portuguese. He possessed an intuitive knowledge of the best way to deal with Asiatic peoples. He understood the importance of pomp and ceremony, and the influence exerted by the possession of the prestige of victory.

Throughout there was something of the grandiose in his nature and his views. His project of establishing an empire in India naturally seemed absurd to his contemporaries. And the attempt to realise it exhausted the Portuguese nation. But the existence of the English empire in India has shown that Albuquerque's idea was not impracticable in itself; it was his nation which proved inadequate to the task. Albuquerque's courage and his cruelty, his piety and his cunning, were not peculiar to himself; they were shared by other men of his time and country. But his tenacity of purpose, his broadminded tolerance, and his statesmanlike views were absolutely unique, and helped to win for him his proud designation of Affonso de Albuquerque the Great.

CHAPTER VII

THE SUCCESSORS OF ALBUQUERQUE: NUNO DA CUNHA AND DOM JOÃO DE CASTRO

It is not intended in this volume to give a complete history of the Portuguese in India. But it is both interesting and instructive to examine the policy of the successors of Albuquerque, and to note the growth of the causes which led to the destruction of the empire that he founded. The following chapters are intended to give a short sketch of the leading features of the history of the Portuguese in India, up to the time when Portugal lost its independence and was united with Spain. Special attention will be given to the points in which Albuquerque's successors fulfilled or diverged from his ideas of conquest and government.

Albuquerque's immediate successor, who had been sent out to supersede him, was Lopo Soares de Albergaria, a powerful nobleman and son of the Chancellor of Portugal. He came out to India with the express intention of striking out a line for himself, and his favourite counsellors were the declared opponents of his predecessor. Nevertheless he dared not abandon Goa, much as that measure was urged upon him, in the face of the marked approval that the King had expressed on the receipt of the important despatch by Albuquerque, which has been printed in full. The new Governor knew that the only way in which he could obtain the favour of Emmanuel was by carrying out the policy of closing the Red Sea. It has been said that the King of Portugal had eventually decided to leave this task in Albuquerque's hands, and that these instructions only reached India after the death of the great captain.

Lopo Soares attempted to fulfil the designs of Albuquerque, and in 1517 sailed with a fleet of over forty ships carrying 3000 soldiers to the Red Sea. This armament, which far exceeded any that Albuquerque had ever commanded, could easily have accomplished the favourite scheme of King Emmanuel. The politics of the Red Sea were become very complicated since Albuquerque's voyage thither. The Emir Husain on leaving India had betaken himself to Jeddah, where he was endeavouring to construct a fresh fleet. But the Sultan of Egypt suspected the Emir's intentions, and ordered an officer named Rais Suláimán to establish his authority in the Red Sea. Suláimán equipped a fleet at Suez, and in 1516 attempted to take Aden. The Arab ruler of that port resisted the Egyptians as sturdily as he had done the Portuguese, and the Egyptian admiral was forced to retreat. The rivalry between Suláimán and Husain weakened the position of the Muhammadans in the Red Sea. When, therefore, Lopo Soares with his great armament approached

Aden, the Arab ruler, feeling it impossible to resist, owing to the breaches in the fortifications made by the Egyptians, offered to surrender his city to the Portuguese commander. It seems hardly conceivable that Albuquerque's successor rejected the offer, but so it was. Lopo Soares thought he would be doing better service by keeping his forces together and sailing to the attack of one or both of the Muhammadan admirals. But the fates fought against him. Storms scattered his fleet; famine and disease decimated his men; and the captains, now that the strong hand of Albuquerque was removed, were utterly insubordinate.

When the Portuguese Governor got back to Aden he found that the defences had been repaired, and that the Arabs were not inclined to repeat their former offer. With his diminished and dispirited force he dared not attack, and he sailed away to India. On his arrival Lopo Soares found that a high civil official had been sent out from Portugal to take charge of judicial and administrative duties, who was to hold a position independent to the governor. Lopo Soares declined to recognise the new authority, and its first tenant was sent back to Portugal. Though Albuquerque's immediate successor had failed in the Red Sea, he took one important step for the furtherance of Portuguese commerce and dominion. He sailed to the island of Ceylon in 1518 and constructed a fortress in the neighbourhood of Colombo. This was the first step towards the conquest of Ceylon, which was afterwards to be one of the most wealthy and important possessions of the Portuguese in the East.

Diogo Lopes de Sequeira, the discoverer of Malacca, who succeeded Lopo Soares in 1518, and Dom Duarte de Menezes, who held office from 1521 to 1524, did not leave much mark on the history of the Portuguese in the East. The most important event which occurred during their rule in India was the death of King Emmanuel in 1521. The sagacity of this monarch had done much to develop the Asiatic empire of Portugal. He had chosen his men wisely, and had perceived quickly the most important obstacles in the way; he had not spared money, ships or forces to develop his new dominions; and he had had the wisdom, for some years at any rate, to leave Albuquerque untrammelled, though he had made the mistake of superseding him at the last. Yet Emmanuel does not deserve very great credit. It was his predecessor, John II, who had directed the explorations which led to such great results, and who had trained the statesmen and captains who achieved those results. Emmanuel showed by his internal policy in Portugal that he was not a great king; his one dream was to secure the thrones of Spain; for this reason he had married in succession two of the daughters of Ferdinand and Isabella; and for this purpose he had consented, at their request, to expel the Jews, to whose commercial enterprise Portugal owed much, from his dominions. Personally he was an ungrateful and a suspicious ruler. He never employed Vasco da Gama after his second voyage in 1502, and he kept the profits of the commerce which had been opened for Portugal strictly to himself.

John III, Emmanuel's successor, was a more estimable man than Emmanuel; he knew how to recognise and reward ability and valour. But he had one defect which proved fatal to the Portuguese power in Asia: he was a fanatical bigot. He looked upon the Portuguese connection with the East not only as a lucrative monopoly to increase the wealth of the Crown, but as an opportunity for spreading Christianity among the heathen. He sent out missionaries as his father had sent soldiers; he established the Holy Inquisition in Portugal which sapped the intellect and vigour of the Portuguese nation; and it was directly due to his example that the fatal policy of religious persecution was introduced into India as a branch of Christianity.

The first selection which John III made for the government of the Portuguese in Asia was an act of reparation. On his accession to the throne he created Dom Vasco da Gama Count of Vidigueira, and in 1523 he appointed the discoverer of the direct sea route to India to the office of Viceroy, which had not been held since the days of Dom Francisco de Almeida. This title carried with it more extensive powers than were exercised by Albuquerque and his next successors. Such powers were sorely needed. Complaints came yearly from India of the oppression and the peculation of the Portuguese officials in the East. They made use of their positions to pile up fortunes for themselves, and charges of corruption were even brought against the Governor.

Under these circumstances a man of strong character and high rank was needed to remedy such abuses, and no fitter man could be found than the illustrious admiral of the Indian Seas, Dom Vasco da Gama. He justified the opinion held of him by the king. He reached Chaul, where Sequeira had built a fortress, in September 1524; he at once proceeded to Goa, where he degraded the Captain, Francisco Pereira Pestana, and directed that his property should be sequestrated until all charges against him were heard. He then went on to Cochin, and there demanded and received the resignation of the Governor, Dom Duarte de Menezes, on the return of the latter from Ormuz. These salutary examples had a great effect. But the Viceroy was too old to thoroughly reform the abuses which had sprung up. He only held office for four months, and died at Cochin on Christmas Eve, 1524. The great navigator was buried in the Chapel of the Franciscan friars at Cochin, but in 1538 his bones were removed to Portugal, and were interred at Vidigueira.

When Vasco da Gama was sent to India as Viceroy a new custom was inaugurated for the succession of governors. Hitherto much inconvenience had been caused by the interregnum which followed on the death or departure of a governor. Vasco da Gama therefore carried with him sealed packets containing in order the names of those whom the King nominated to succeed him. The care of the sealed packets was entrusted to the high civil official who held the title of Controller (Veador) of Indian affairs and had complete charge of administrative and judicial matters. Lopo Soares had refused to recognise this official, but the King insisted on the creation of the office, and took effective means to secure its entire independence of the governors.

On Vasco da Gama's death the first sealed packet was found to contain the name of Dom Henrique de Menezes, who had won golden opinions as Pestana's successor at Goa. This young nobleman died at Cannanore on February 21st, 1526. The name contained in the next sealed packet was that of Pedro Mascarenhas, who was at this time Captain of Malacca. As he could not arrive for some months, the third packet was then opened, which contained the name of Lopo Vaz de Sam

Paio, Captain of Cochin and a former officer of Albuquerque. Frequent complaints were sent to Portugal of the harshness and corruption of this Governor. It is asserted that he was incapable as well as cruel, and that the Portuguese fortresses were in a disgraceful state of neglect. He treated even the royal orders with contempt, and refused to hand over the government to Pedro Mascarenhas, whom he ordered into custody on his return from Malacca to claim his rights.

It was further made known to John III that Suláimán the Magnificent was setting on foot a great fleet for India. This was mainly due to the constant requests of the Venetians who were being ruined by the Portuguese monopoly, and was in general accordance with the policy of the greatest of the Ottoman rulers of Constantinople. The war between the Turks and Egyptians, which had allowed the Portuguese to develop in Asia, ended in 1517 with the overthrow of the Mameluke dynasty in Egypt. This great conquest of the Sultan Selim brought with it the submission of Syria and Arabia. Suláimán the Magnificent succeeded his father Selim in 1520, and began his reign by his famous campaigns in Hungary and against Rhodes. He was quite alive to the importance to Islám of checking the further advance of the Portuguese in the East, and the news that he was building a great fleet at Suez was perfectly true. It was placed under the command of Suláimán Pasha, and carried many Venetian and Christian adventurers as well as Turks and Egyptians.

Such being the dangers which threatened the Portuguese empire in Asia, John III selected to meet them the first really great successor to the office of Albuquerque, Nuno da Cunha. The new Governor was the eldest son of Tristão da Cunha, the navigator, and had had a large experience of Asiatic warfare. He was knighted by his relative, the great Albuquerque, in 1506, and had ever since been employed in voyages to the East and in hard-fought campaigns in Morocco. His chief feat of arms up to this time had been his conquest of Mombassa on the African coast in 1525, which he had followed up by exacting the tribute promised by the King of Ormuz to the Portuguese.

He left Lisbon in 1528 with a large fleet, carrying 4000 soldiers. He reached Goa in October, 1529, after a long voyage, and at once arrested Lopo Vaz de Sam Paio, and sent him back to Portugal in chains. His first measures were directed to the reform of internal abuses. With great activity he visited every Portuguese factory and fortress, punishing all evil-doers, and setting himself a noble example of personal probity. But he was not satisfied, like his predecessors, by merely securing old advantages and maintaining the former centres of trade. He devoted himself to opening up new provinces and developing the Portuguese commerce and dominion in other parts of India. The first Portuguese settlement on the Coromandel coast was at Saint Thomé near Madras, which received that name from the supposed discovery of the bones of St. Thomas the apostle of India. But Nuno da Cunha pushed farther up the coast and opened up a political connection with the wealthy province of Bengal.

Hitherto the Portuguese relations with Bengal had been purely commercial. In 1518 the first Portuguese ship, commanded by João da Silveira, reached Chittagong, and he there found João Coelho, who had arrived some months before from Malacca, having explored the eastern coast of the Bay of Bengal in a native craft. Silveira took a rich cargo on board, and after his visit it became an established custom for a Portuguese ship to visit Chittagong every year to purchase merchandise for Portugal. But Nuno da Cunha wished to do more than this, and to establish a regular factory and a political influence in the richest province of India.

An opportunity was afforded him in 1534, when the Muhammadan King of Bengal asked for the help of a Portuguese force against the Afghán invader, Sher Sháh. Nuno da Cunha promised his assistance, and at once sent a fleet of nine ships, carrying 400 Portuguese soldiers under the command of Martim Affonso de Mello Jusarte. The Portuguese contingent behaved gallantly, and its deeds are described in the first twelve chapters of the ninth Book of the fourth Decade of João de Barros, the contemporary Portuguese historian. Nuno da Cunha intended to follow in person, but he was prevented by the condition of affairs in Gujarát. It happened therefore that Portuguese authority was never directly established in Bengal. No royal factory or fortress was erected, and the Portuguese settlement at Húglí, where goods were collected for shipment to Portugal, was loosely considered to be subject to the Captain of Ceylon. The Portuguese in North-Eastern India remained to the end adventurers and merchants, and were never a ruling power.

The important events which prevented Nuno da Cunha from visiting Bengal were closely connected with the threatened approach of Suláimán the Magnificent's fleet from the Red Sea. It was well understood that that fleet would sail direct to the coast of Gujarát as the fleet of Emir Husain had done thirty years before. This knowledge made Nuno da Cunha very anxious to establish the Portuguese in a strong position on the coasts of North-Western India. Their main station in this neighbourhood had hitherto been the port of Chaul, where they had a factory and a small fortress. Portuguese agents were likewise established in the ports of Gujarát, but they were in no place masters of a strong defensive position.

To obtain a fitting site for a fortress in Gujarát was a principal aim of Nuno da Cunha's policy; not only for defence against the Muhammadans in India, but also as a bulwark against the expected Turkish fleet. Circumstances favoured him. The Mughal Emperor Humáyún was engaged in war with Bahádur Sháh, the King of Ahmadábád or Gujarát. In his extremity Bahádur Sháh sought to make an alliance with the Portuguese, and for this purpose he granted them the island of Bassein, which was then separated from the mainland by a narrow creek. Bassein lies about twenty-eight miles north of Bombay, and afterwards became the northern capital of Portuguese India, almost rivalling Goa in splendour and prosperity. At Bassein the Portuguese built a fort, but the place was not naturally defensible, and Nuno da Cunha set his heart on the possession of the rocky island of Diu, which had been one of the spots designed by Albuquerque for a Portuguese stronghold.

At last, in 1535, under the pressure of an invasion by Humáyún, Bahádur Sháh allowed the Portuguese to erect a fortress in Diu and to garrison it with their own troops. The fortress was rapidly and solidly built, and Bahádur Sháh and Nuno da Cunha signed a treaty of alliance. Such an alliance was not likely to last, and the murder of Bahádur Sháh in 1537, which took place on his return from visiting Nuno da Cunha on board his ship, caused a cry of treachery to be raised. It seems absolutely certain that the death of the King of Gujarát was due to a misunderstanding, but none the less friendship was owing to it replaced by bitter enmity. The fortress was not completed a moment too soon, for in 1538 the Turkish fleet, under Suláimán Pasha, after taking Aden by a stratagem, blockaded Diu by sea. Muhammad III, the nephew and successor of Bahádur Sháh, then besieged the place by land.

Antonio da Silveira, who had been left by Nuno da Cunha as Captain of the fortress, defended it nobly. Brilliant are the feats of gallantry recorded by the Portuguese chroniclers on the part not only of the soldiers but of aged men, boys, and women. The siege lasted many months, during which Nuno da Cunha was succeeded in September 1538 by Dom Garcia de Noronha, Albuquerque's nephew, who had been sent out from Portugal as Viceroy. This experienced officer managed to introduce reinforcements into the fortress in small boats which slipped between the great Turkish galleys. Every assault was repulsed, and in November 1538 Suláimán Pasha and Muhammad III abandoned the siege. It does not detract from the glory of Silveira's defence that its final success was mainly due to dissensions among the besiegers. Each of the Muhammadan commanders blamed the other; the King of Gujarát began to fear that the Turkish admiral would attack him, and it was with a sense of relief that he, as well as the Portuguese, saw Suláimán sail away to Arabia.

It was a melancholy fact that Nuno da Cunha was unable to witness the success of his brother-in-law, Silveira. In spite of his great services he, like his relative Affonso de Albuquerque, whom he resembled in his wide views and his personal disinterestedness, was slandered at the Court of Lisbon. He had taken harsh measures against embezzling officials and insubordinate captains, and during his ten years of government he made numerous enemies. These men persuaded the King that Nuno da Cunha was making a large fortune, when really he was spending his private property for the public service; and, in spite of the arguments of old Tristão da Cunha, Dom Garcia de Noronha was ordered to send the greatest Portuguese Governor of India since Albuquerque home in custody. On his way home Nuno da Cunha died at sea on March 5, 1539, in the fifty-second year of his age, and his last words, when his chaplain asked what should be done with his body, were: 'Since the will of God is that I should die at sea, let the sea be my grave; for since the land will not have me why should I leave my bones to it.' Nuno da Cunha's establishment of the Portuguese at Diu was the most important event since the conquest of Goa; in temper and in disposition he resembled his great relative; like Albuquerque, he was treated with ingratitude and died in disgrace.

Dom Garcia de Noronha did not rule long enough to affect the history of the Portuguese in India. He died at Goa on April 3, 1540, and was succeeded as Governor, not as Viceroy, by Dom Estevão da Gama, the second son of the famous navigator. The new governor was an experienced officer; he had been Captain of the Sea during his father's short viceroyalty in 1524; had made more than one voyage to India; and had acted for five years as Captain of Malacca.

The one remarkable event of his governorship was his expedition to the Red Sea. The repulse of Suláimán Pasha had been followed by his death in Arabia, but Suláimán the Magnificent did not intend to abandon his projects, and directed the equipment of a new fleet at Suez. In 1541 Dom Estevão da Gama entered the Red Sea. He was repulsed in an attack on Suez, but made a landing in the neighbourhood and a pilgrimage to the monastery of Mount Sinai, where he knighted some of his officers, including Dom Alvaro de Castro, the son of his most distinguished captain, Dom João de Castro. Before returning to India the Governor sent his brother, Dom Christovão da Gama, to escort a prelate, whom the Pope had nominated as primate of Abyssinia. But the Christian dynasty in that country was at this time hotly beset by the Muhammadans, and Dom Christovão was killed with his companions.

In the year 1542 Dom Estevão da Gama was succeeded as Governor by Martim Affonso de Sousa, who had shown ability in the exploration and settlement of the colony of Brazil. De Sousa's government of India was not very successful. His most notable achievement was a treaty with Ibráhím Adil Sháh, King of Bijápur, who promised to cede to the Portuguese the provinces of Bardes and Salsette adjoining the island of Goa in exchange for the surrender of a Muhammadan prince, Mir Ali Khán (Mealecan). But Martim Affonso de Sousa had neither the ability nor the authority to maintain his influence over his own captains, and King John III resolved to send to India a nobleman of military experience, who by his rank and his character should restore harmony in his Asiatic possessions.

The nobleman selected was Dom João de Castro, who was the intimate friend of the King's brother Dom Luis. With that prince he had served in the expedition against Tunis, where his conspicuous valour had won the admiration of the Emperor Charles V. He displayed courage, tact, and self-reliance, both in the relief of Diu and in the campaign of 1541 in the Red Sea. But it was for the purity of his personal character, the integrity of his life, and his absolute honesty that he was specially selected.

Enormous fortunes were being made in the East, and the usual abuses accompanied the rapid acquisition of wealth. Bribery and corruption in public life, gambling and immorality in private life had reached an alarming height, and though the Portuguese still exhibited the same valour and constancy in war as in the days of Albuquerque, they were now too apt to prefer private advantage to the good of the State. Dom João de Castro took out with him a powerful fleet and 2000 soldiers, and he was accompanied by two young sons, Dom Alvaro and Dom Fernão, who rivalled in the East the glory of the youthful Dom Lourenço de Almeida and of Albuquerque's young nephew Dom Antonio de Noronha.

Dom João de Castro reached Goa on September 10, 1545, and at once took over the charge of the government. He found himself face to face with two serious dangers; Ibráhím Adil Sháh of Bijápur was preparing to attack Goa, and Muhammad III of Gujarát was again besieging Diu. These were but symptoms of a general league which was in act of formation between all the sovereigns of the West of India against the Portuguese. In spite of the expostulation of the officials João de Castro refused to carry out the engagement made with the King of Bijápur by his predecessor. He declared that Mir Ali Khán had come to seek refuge at Goa, and that it would be a most dishonourable act to surrender him. The King of Bijápur at once sent an army to recover the provinces of Bardes and Salsette, which he had handed over, but Dom João de Castro marched out and inflicted a severe defeat on the Bijápur forces.

The situation at Diu was more threatening. A renegade Albanian, called by the Portuguese Coge Çofar (Khoja Zufar), had attained supreme influence at the Court of Muhammad III of Gujarát. He persuaded the King that it was most disgraceful for him to fail in capturing Diu. He collected the whole force of the kingdom and commenced the siege of the Portuguese fortress, with the declaration that he would die sooner than return unsuccessful. The Captain of Diu, Dom João Mascarenhas, showed the same constancy and valour as Antonio da Silveira. The garrison consisted of nearly the same soldiers, and the women once more distinguished themselves in the defence. The Governor made every effort to relieve the fortress. He first sent his son, Dom Fernão, who was killed, then his other son, Dom Alvaro, and eventually brought up all the forces he could collect in person. Coge Çofar was slain by a cannon-ball, and his successor, Rumecão, did not press the siege with the same vigour.

After repulsing all assaults, Dom João de Castro marched out at the head of his army and utterly defeated the enemy in a pitched battle. The slaughter among the Muhammadans was immense, and the victory was one of the greatest ever won by a European army in India. He then proceeded to punish the Gujarátís. One of his captains, Antonio Moniz Barreto, burnt Cambay, and his son, Dom Alvaro, sacked Surat. This great victory showed the native princes that they had a worthy successor of Albuquerque to deal with, and Dom João de Castro was on all sides entreated to make alliances with them. With the King of Bijápur alone the war continued, but the Portuguese everywhere got the best of it; Dábhol was taken, and the Muhammadans were again defeated on land.

The internal reforms were even more to the credit of Dom João de Castro than his victories. One point in his policy resembles that adopted by Cornwallis in Bengal; namely, the fixing of the salaries of the various officials, and his effort to put an end to the system of peculation which was rife. This peculation was chiefly caused by the officials engaging in trade; by which they made vast profits while the State suffered. The state of things had partly arisen through the custom of allowing Portuguese soldiers to trade after serving for nine years. It was this inducement which brought so many soldiers from Portugal; and in spite of the Governor's representations, the Portuguese authorities were afraid to put an end to it for fear of stopping the flow of recruits. The reforming measures of Dom João de Castro did not remain long in operation, but his example had a great effect. So great was the confidence felt in his probity, that an anecdote is told of his raising money in Goa for the relief of Diu, by pawning the hairs of his beard.

The news of Dom João de Castro's victory at Diu was received with great enthusiasm by John III, who in 1548 sent him a commission as Viceroy. He only lived to hold this high office for fourteen days. He died at Goa on June 6, 1548, in the arms of his friend, the Apostle to the Indies, Saint Francis Xavier. The greatest of all the successors of Albuquerque was Dom João de Castro; he resembled the knights of the middle ages in his gallantry and his disinterestedness, while his victory at Diu is the last great achievement of the Portuguese arms in Asia.

CHAPTER VIII

THE SUCCESSORS OF ALBUQUERQUE (CONTINUED): DOM CONSTANTINO DE BRAGANZA AND DOM LUIS DE ATHAIDE

The thirty-five years which followed from the death of Dom João de Castro to the extinction of the independence of Portugal are neither so interesting nor so important as those which saw the building up of the Portuguese power in the East. Commercially, the value of Vasco da Gama's voyage and of Albuquerque's victories became greater than ever. The largest fleets of merchant-ships ever sent to Portugal were despatched after Philip II of Spain had become also Philip I of Portugal. The Portuguese monopoly remained unbroken until 1595, and the nations of Europe, while they grew in civilisation and in love of luxury, continued until that time to buy from Lisbon the Asiatic commodities which had become necessary to them. As the commerce became systematised it grew larger and more profitable, both to the Royal Treasury which equipped the merchant fleets and sold their cargoes at Lisbon, and to the individual agents in India, who purchased the goods which made up these cargoes. But politically the history of the Portuguese in India becomes less interesting. There were no more great discoveries; no more great conquests and great victories; no more grandiose conceptions of expelling the Muhammadans from the markets of Asia.

Gallant feats of arms were still accomplished, but they only proved how the Portuguese had degenerated since the days of Albuquerque. The defence of Goa by Dom Luis de Athaide was brilliant, but after all it was a defensive operation, and not a victory such as Dom João de Castro had won at Diu, or the storming of a strong city, like the captures of Goa and Malacca by Albuquerque. There were one or two high-minded and able men among the successors of the splendid Albuquerque, but they did not attempt to rival his deeds or carry out his ideas. The romance of Portuguese history in the East is no longer bound up with the growth of the power of the nation, but is to be found rather in the careers of daring adventurers such as Fernão Mendes Pinto and Sebastião Gonzales. The complete attainment of commercial prosperity seems to have destroyed the dream of Empire.

But at the time when the political interest in the career of the Portuguese in Asia diminishes, the religious interest increases. The new heroes of Portugal are not her soldiers and her sailors, but her missionaries. These were the men who made their way into the interior of India, and who penetrated the farthest East. Japan, China, and even Tibet, witnessed their presence and heard their preaching; the great Emperor Akbar gave them a not unkindly welcome at his Court at Agra; and they laboured among the savages of the Spice Islands as well as among the learned men of China and of India.

The greatest of all these missionaries, Saint Francis Xavier, was not a Portuguese subject. But the Company of Jesus, of which he was the pioneer missionary, contained many Portuguese, and he could not have attempted what he did but for the support of the Portuguese government at home and of the Portuguese authorities in India.

The idea of discouraging Christian missionaries, which formed a part of the policy of the Dutch and English East India Companies, never had an adherent among the Portuguese. They believed sincerely in their religion, and the principal use they made of their influence when they were firmly established in Asia was to spread it abroad. Again and again orders were sent from Portugal that the missionaries were to be assisted in every possible way.

The Franciscan friars who first came to India were engaged in looking after the souls of the Portuguese soldiers, but they were followed, and in increasing numbers after the successes of Saint Francis, by priests and friars and Jesuits, who left Europe for the express purpose of converting the heathen. The history of the Roman Catholic missions in India, for which there is plenty of material, would need a volume in itself. It must suffice to point out that those missions did not begin to attain their full development until after the Portuguese had reached their highest political power during the governorship of Dom João de Castro, and were beginning to decline.

In 1538 the Pope nominated for the first time a Bishop of Goa in the person of Frei João de Albuquerque, a Franciscan friar, and a relative of the great Governor. This holy man, who won a great reputation for sanctity, died in 1553, and in 1557 the see of Goa was raised to an archbishopric and conferred upon Dom Gaspar de Leão Pereira. The archbishops soon rivalled the viceroys in wealth and dignity, and in at least one instance, at the beginning of the seventeenth century, an archbishop also acted as governor. Other sees were speedily established at Cochin, Malacca, and Macão, and many missionary bishops were appointed for other parts of India, China, and Japan. The first labourers in the mission field were the Franciscans. They were soon followed by other religious orders, and were exceeded in success and ability by the Jesuits.

In 1560, after the death of Dom João de Castro and of St. Francis Xavier, the Holy Inquisition was established in Goa. It was granted as its headquarters the magnificent palace of Yusaf Adil Sháh, which had been the residence of the viceroys until 1554. Its first action was rather corrective than persecuting, and it was not until the seventeenth century that the periodical burnings of relapsed converts and supposed witches, which are known as *Autos da Fé,* commenced their sanguinary work. The most notable event in the religious history of the Portuguese in India, the condemnation of the doctrines and ritual of the Nestorian Christians of the Malabar coast, did not occur till the Synod of Diamper (Udayampura) in 1599.

The educational work of the missionaries, their custom of dwelling among the people and imitating their mode of life, as well as their building of superb churches in the Portuguese cities, well deserve an extended notice, which cannot be adequately given in this volume. It is enough to say that Albuquerque, though zealous and desirous of spreading the faith, did not initiate the policy of persecution. It was his feeble successors who threw away the opportunity afforded for the propagation of the Christian faith, by the existence of a native Christian community in the very part of India where the Portuguese first landed.

When the sealed order of succession was opened, after the lamented death of Dom João de Castro, it was found that the two first nominees, Dom João Mascarenhas and Dom Jorge Tello de Menezes, had already left India for Portugal. The third packet opened contained the name of Garcia de Sá, an aged gentleman, who had spent nearly all his life in India. He hastened to make peace with Ibráhím Adil Sháh of Bijápur, and with Muhammad III of Gujarát. To the former he promised that the Portuguese would not allow Mir Ali Khán to leave Goa, and on that condition the cession of Bardes and Salsette was confirmed. In the treaty with the King of Gujarát it was agreed that the Portuguese should continue to hold the fortress of Diu, which they had twice so gallantly defended, while the city and the rest of the island remained subject to Muhammad III. Garcia de Sá died at Goa on July 13, 1549, and was succeeded as governor by Jorge Cabral, a descendant of the second Portuguese captain who visited India.

Cabral, who was Captain of Bassein, assumed the office and engaged in a war that was raging between the Rájá of Cochin and the Zamorin. He had taken and sacked Tiracol and Ponáni, and was just about to attack Calicut, when he received information of the arrival of Dom Affonso de Noronha as Viceroy. This nobleman was the second son of the Marquis de Villa Real, and had been selected for the office of Viceroy by John III, though no Viceroy had been sent out from Portugal with full powers since Dom Garcia de Noronha in 1538. The Viceroy, on taking over office from Cabral, declined to attack Calicut and ordered the fleet back to Goa. He ruled for four years, during which time he greatly extended the Portuguese power in the island of Ceylon.

Dom Affonso de Noronha was succeeded as Viceroy in 1554 by Dom Pedro Mascarenhas, an aged nobleman who had filled the office of ambassador to the Emperor Charles V and the Pope, and had since acted as governor to the heir-apparent. He was over seventy years of age when he was sent to India, and held office but nine months. On his death the sealed orders were opened, and the first name found in them was that of Francisco Barreto, a most experienced officer. This governor is chiefly known from his persecution of the poet Camoens, whom he sent to the little island of Macão as a punishment for a satire he had written on the pride and immorality of the officials at Goa. But Barreto was a very vigorous governor. He did much to strengthen the various Portuguese fortresses throughout Asia, and showed himself a skilful and daring general.

During Barreto's government King John III of Portugal died, leaving the throne to his infant grandson, the ill-fated King Sebastian. One of the first acts of the widow of John III, Queen Catherine, who became Regent of the kingdom, was to appoint a prince of the blood royal, Dom Constantino de Braganza, to be Viceroy. This young prince was only thirty years of age, but he soon showed that he surpassed his predecessors in ability as well as in rank. He reached Goa in 1558, and one of his earliest measures was to capture Damán, where he erected a fortress. This place and Goa and Diu are at the present time the only relics of the Portuguese power in India. On his return from Damán he dispatched powerful fleets to Malacca, to Ormuz, and to Ceylon, and placed the position of affairs in all parts of Asia in a most favourable condition for the Portuguese.

Dom Constantino de Braganza's internal reforms resembled those of João de Castro; he endeavoured to put down peculation, and insisted on the obedience of his officers. In 1560 he made an expedition with a powerful armament to Ceylon, where he took Jaffnapatam, which became the capital of the Portuguese power in that island. The high character of the young prince, no less than his courage and his enterprise, caused the Rájás of India to treat him with great respect, and he was begged by the Queen Regent to continue in office, and even to accept the post of Viceroy of India for life. He refused, and in 1561 was succeeded as Viceroy by Dom Francisco de Coutinho, Count of Redondo.

After the resignation of Dom Constantino de Braganza few events of importance happened for some years to the Portuguese in India. The Muhammadan King of Bijápur, Ali Adil Sháh, who had succeeded his father Ibráhím in 1557, was at first more concerned with his scheme to break the power of the last great Hindu sovereign, the Rájá of Vijayanagar, than to attack the Portuguese. Freed from danger on this side, the Portuguese governors were able to scatter their power over small but successful expeditions. The most notable of these was to Ceylon, which was gradually brought entirely under the control of the Portuguese. The Count of Redondo died in March, 1564, at Goa, and was succeeded as Viceroy, after a short administration as Governor by João de Mendonça, by Dom Antão de Noronha.

The new Viceroy commenced his government by the capture of Mangalore, but the important events which occurred during his tenure of office took place without his active intervention. The first of these was the siege of Malacca by the King of Achin. The defence of Albuquerque's conquest ranks with that of Diu. It is true that the savage Achinese were not such formidable soldiers as the Turks or the Gujarátís; but, on the other hand, Malacca was further from Goa, and it was more difficult to obtain reinforcements. The Captain who maintained the defence was Dom Leonis Pereira, who held out for several months and eventually beat off his enemies after killing more than 4000 of them.

The other event was the defeat of the Rájá of Vijayanagar in 1565, at Tálikot, by the allied Muhammadan kings of the Deccan. It may fairly be conjectured that Albuquerque would have assisted the last powerful Hindu monarch against the Muhammadans, for it was a part of his policy to pose as the protector of the Hindus. But his successors did not appreciate his policy, and, disgusted by an attack which the Hindu prince had made some years previously on the Portuguese settlement of Saint Thomé, they left the Rájá of Vijayanagar to his fate.

In 1568 Dom Luis de Athaide, an officer who had had much experience in Indian warfare, and who had been knighted as a lad by Dom Estevão da Gama in the monastery of Mount Sinai, arrived in Goa as Viceroy. He quickly perceived that a first result of the victory of Tálikot must be that the King of Bijápur would attack Goa. The city of Goa had far outgrown the limits imposed by the wall which Albuquerque had built. Dom Antão de Noronha had, during his government, begun to build a new wall, which was to run from the north-eastern angle of the island of Goa and should terminate at the west of the city. Dom Luis de Athaide continued this wall, and was in the act of building other fortifications when Ali Adil Sháh declared war and made his way into the island with an army estimated at 100,000 men, and accompanied by more than 2000 elephants. This attack was part of a general scheme formed by the Muhammadan rulers of India, with the Zamorin of Calicut and the King of Achin, to expel the Portuguese from Asia. Even sovereigns who had hitherto been allies of the Portuguese, such as the Rájá of Honáwar, joined in the league against them.

Never was the situation of the Portuguese more critical; never did they show more conspicuous valour. The garrison of Goa, when the siege commenced in 1570, only consisted of 700 Portuguese soldiers. Consequently the Viceroy placed under arms 300 friars and priests and about a thousand slaves. The defence was worthy of the best days of the Portuguese power. For ten months an obstinate resistance was offered, and at the end of that time Ali Adil Sháh retreated, having lost by disease and by fighting the larger part of his army.

The defence of Goa, by the Viceroy, was rivalled by the gallant resistance of Malacca, of Chaul, and of Chalé near Calicut, where Dom Leonis Pereira, Dom Jorge de Menezes, and Dom Diogo de Menezes, all repulsed their assailants. On the retreat of Ali Adil Sháh from before Goa, the Portuguese Viceroy swept the Malabar coast, punishing all opponents and relieving the other garrisons. His vengeance was particularly shown at Honáwar, which he burnt. Just after the league was finally broken, on September 7, 1571, Dom Antonio de Noronha arrived to succeed Dom Luis de Athaide as Viceroy. The defender of Goa received a cordial welcome on his return to Lisbon from his friend, the young King Sebastian, who created him Count of Atouguia.

Dom Antonio de Noronha, who was only a distant relative of the predecessor of Dom Luis de Athaide, did not possess the powers of previous Viceroys. King Sebastian perceived the great inconvenience of leaving the whole of his possessions from the Cape of Good Hope to Japan under the superintendence of the Goa government. The difficulty of communication was so great that for months at a time the captains of the more distant settlements were practically independent. It was resolved, therefore, to divide the East into three independent governorships.

Dom Antonio de Noronha, with the title of Viceroy, was to be supreme from the coasts of Arabia to Ceylon, with his capital at Goa. This left him entire control of the Indian and Persian trade. Antonio Moniz Barreto was to govern from Bengal to the furthest East, with his headquarters at Malacca, and was charged with the control of the spice trade. Francisco Barreto, the former Governor of India, was to rule all the Portuguese settlements on the South-East coast of Africa, with his capital at Mozambique.

Hitherto these African settlements had been regarded solely as stopping-places for the fleets to and from India. But King Sebastian wished to use them also as the basis for exploration and conquest in the interior of Africa. This is not a history of the Portuguese in Africa, but it may be remarked that much important and interesting work was done by the Portuguese in that continent during the sixteenth century which seems to be forgotten by writers on the opening up of Africa at the present time. Francisco Barreto, for instance, made his way far into the interior and conquered the kingdom and city of Monomotapa, where he died.

Dom Antonio de Noronha handed over the government of India in 1573 to Antonio Moniz Barreto. Ruy Lourenço de Tavora, who was nominated to succeed as Viceroy, died on his way out, and Dom Diogo de Menezes, the defender of Chalé, administered the government from 1576 to 1578. He was superseded by Dom Luis de Athaide, who at the special request of King Sebastian consented once more to return to India. Athaide's second viceroyalty was not marked by any important event. He died at Goa on March 10, 1581; it is said from a broken heart caused by the news of the defeat of the King Sebastian and of his melancholy death at Alcacer Quibir (El-Kasr Kebir) in Morocco.

With the death of Dom Luis de Athaide this rapid sketch of the successors of Albuquerque must end: he was the last great Portuguese ruler in the East, and none of the Viceroys who succeeded him deserve separate notice. The commercial monopoly of Portugal lasted some years longer, but the fabric of the Portuguese power in India was utterly rotten, and gave way with hardly a struggle before the first assaults of the Dutch merchant-adventurers.

The causes of the rapid fall of Portuguese influence in Asia are as interesting to examine as the causes of their rapid success, and, like the latter, they may be classed under external and internal headings. The chief external cause was the union of the Portuguese crown with that of Spain in 1580. Philip II kept the promise he made to the Cortes of Thomar, and appointed none but Portuguese to offices in Portuguese Asia. His accession to the throne was everywhere recognised in the East, and the Prior of Crato who opposed him found no adherents there. The first Viceroy whom Philip nominated, Dom Francisco Mascarenhas, bore a name famous in Portugal, and had no difficulty in persuading the various captains of fortresses to swear fealty to the Spanish king. It is curious to note among the Viceroys whom Philip II nominated to Goa two relations of the most famous Portuguese conquerors in the East, Mathias de Albuquerque and Dom Francisco da Gama, grandson of the navigator. In spite of Philip's loyalty in this respect, the fact that he was King of Portugal involved that country in war with the Dutch and the English. The merchants of Amsterdam and London were forbidden to come to Lisbon for Asiatic commodities, and they consequently resolved to go to the East and get them for themselves. In 1595 the first Dutch fleet doubled the Cape of Good Hope, and in 1601 it was followed by the first English fleet, both being despatched by trading companies. The Portuguese endeavoured to expel the intruders, but they signally failed.

The reasons for this failure are to be found in the internal causes of the Portuguese decline. The union with Spain brought their rivals into the Eastern seas, but it was their own weakness which let those rivals triumph. The primary cause of that weakness was the complete exhaustion of the Portuguese nation. Year after year this little country, which never exceeded 3,000,000 in population, sent forth fleets to the East, carrying sometimes as many as 3000 and 4000 soldiers. Of these men few ever returned to Europe. Many perished in battle, in shipwreck, or from the climate, and those who survived were encouraged to settle down and marry native women. During the whole of the sixteenth century Portugal was being drained of men, and those the strongest and bravest of her sons. In return she got plenty of wealth, but money cannot take the place of brain and muscle. Besides becoming exhausted in quantity, the Portuguese in the East rapidly degenerated in quality. It was not only that Albuquerque's successors in supreme command were his inferiors; some of them proved worthy of their office; but the soldiers and sailors and officials showed a lamentable falling off. Brilliant courage was shown up to the siege of Goa in 1570. After that time it is difficult to recognise the heroic Portuguese of Albuquerque's campaigns. Albuquerque's imperial notions were set aside as impracticable, and interest in commerce and in Christian missions took the place of vast schemes of conquest and of empire.

The later history of the Portuguese in Asia may be summed up in a rapid record of their disasters. In 1603 and 1639 the Dutch blockaded Goa. In 1656 they drove the Portuguese from Cannanore; in 1661 from Negapatam and Káyenkolam, the port of Quilon; in 1663 from Cranganore and Cochin. Nor were the Dutch victories confined to India; in 1619 they founded Batavia in the island of Java, and in 1640 they took Malacca and concentrated the whole trade of the Spice Islands at their new settlement. The Dutch were equally successful in Ceylon, which they completely controlled after the capture of Jaffnapatam in 1658. The English were but little later in the field: in 1611 Sir Henry Middleton defeated the Portuguese off Cambay, and in 1615 Captain Best won a great victory over the Portuguese fleet off Swally, the port of Surat. The Dutch and English agencies quickly covered the East, and soon after the middle of the seventeenth century the Asiatic trade of Portugal had practically disappeared. What little commerce survived was in the hands of the Jesuits, and became finally extinct on the suppression of that body by the Marquis of Pombal in 1742.

It was not only by European competitors that the Portuguese power in the East was shattered. It was the Emperor Sháh Jahán who took Húglí in 1629, after an obstinate resistance, and carried away 1000 Portuguese prisoners; and it was Abbas Sháh of Persia, who, with the assistance of some Englishmen, captured Ormuz in 1622. In 1670 a small band of Arabs from Muscat plundered Diu, the fortress which, under Silveira and Mascarenhas, had resisted the utmost power of great Muhammadan fleets and armies.

The Maráthá confederacy also found it easy and profitable to plunder Portuguese settlements in India. In 1739 these hardy Hindu soldiers sacked Bassein, and they extended their incursions to the very walls of Goa. In the eighteenth century a vigorous effort was made by the Portuguese to hold their own with the Maráthás, which met with some success, and led to a considerable increase of the province of Goa. Lastly, it must not be forgotten that in 1661 the Portuguese ceded the island of Bombay to England as part of the dowry of Catherine of Braganza.

The present condition of the Portuguese in India affords a curious commentary on the high aims and great successes of Albuquerque. The remaining Portuguese possessions, Goa, Damán, and Diu could make no pretence of defending themselves against the English Empire in India. They are maintained by Portugal, not for any benefits to be derived from them, but as relics of the past and witnesses to former glory. The condition of the Portuguese is indicated by the treaty which was signed in 1878 with the British Government, by which the right of making salt and the customs duties were ceded to the Government of India for a yearly payment of four lakhs of rupees. This sum was hypothecated for the construction of a railway to Marmagáo, near Goa, which possesses a fine harbour, and will probably increase in wealth as the port of export for the cotton grown in Bellary and the neighbouring British districts.

One interesting relic of the former supremacy of the Portuguese was the right claimed by Portugal to nominate the Roman Catholic prelates throughout India. This right, natural enough in the sixteenth century, became absurd in the nineteenth. A long quarrel arising from this claim has recently been settled by a Concordat between the Pope and the King of Portugal.

The present volume may appropriately close with two descriptions of the Portuguese in India by a Muhammadan and a Hindu writer in the sixteenth century.

> 'The Franks beginning to oppress and commit hostilities against the Muhammadans' says Sheik Zín-ud-dín, in his historical work the *Tohfut-ul-mujahideen,* 'their tyrannical and injurious usage proceeded to a length that was the occasion of a general confusion and distraction amongst the population of the country. This continued for a long period, for nearly eighty years, when the affairs of the Moslems had arrived at the last stage of decay, ruin, poverty and wretchedness; since whilst they were too ill-practised in deceit to dissemble an obedience which was not sincere, they neither possessed the power to repel nor means to evade the evils that afflicted them. Nor did the Muhammadan princes and chieftains who were possessed of large armies, and who had at their command great military resources, come forward for their deliverance or bestow any of their wealth in so holy a cause as in the resistance to these tyrant infidels.' ...[51]
>
> 'Sorely did these Franks oppress the faithful, striving all of them, the great and powerful, the old and young, to eradicate the Muhammadan religion; and to bring over its followers to Christianity (may God ever defend us from such a calamity!). Notwithstanding all this, however, they preserved an outward show of peace towards the Muhammadans, in consequence of their being

[51] *Tohfut-ul-mujahideen,* Rowlandson's translation, pp. 6, 7.

compelled to dwell amongst them; since the chief part of the population of the seaports consisted of Muhammadans ... Lastly it is worthy of remark that the Franks entertain antipathy and hatred only towards Muhammadans, and to their creed alone; evincing no dislike towards the Nairs and other Pagans of similar description.'[52]

In the following terms, according to Dr. Burnell, does Venkatacarya, a Bráhman of Conjevaram, speak about the Portuguese:—

'This Bráhman wrote about A.D. 1600 a Sanskrit poem called Vicvagunadarca, often printed and once rudely translated (Calcutta, 1825, 4to.) In it he mentions the Portuguese, whom he calls Hûna. In abuse of them he says they are very despicable, are devoid of tenderness, and do not value Bráhmans a straw, that they have endless faults, and do not observe ceremonial purity. But he praises their self-restraint and truthfulness, their mechanical skill, and their respect for law.'[53]

Had the Bráhman poet known Albuquerque, or the greatest of his successors, he would have praised also their valour, their tenacity, and their disinterested unselfishness. But striking is the contrast between Albuquerque and even the greatest of his successors. His contemporaries felt this, and his son, in the dedication of the second edition of the *Commentaries* to King Sebastian, in 1574, gives an anecdote which illustrates this general opinion.

'I shall say no more,' he says, 'than tell you what a soldier said who always accompanied him in war. This man being very old and staying in the city of Goa, when he reflected upon the disorder of Indian affairs, went with a stick in his hand to the chapel of Affonso de Albuquerque, and, striking the sepulchre wherein he was lying buried, cried out:—"Oh! great captain, thou hast done me all the harm thou couldst have done, but I cannot deny that thou hast been the greatest conqueror and sufferer of troubles that the world has known: arise thou, for what thou hast gained is like to be lost!"'

[52] *Tohfut-ul-mujahideen,* Rowlandson's translation, pp. 109, 110.

[53] *A Tentative List of Books and some MSS. relating to the History of the Portuguese in India Proper,* by A. C. Burnell, Mangalore, 1880, p. 131.

INDEX

A

B

C

D

E

F

G

H

I

J

K

L

M

Q

R

S

T

Printed by Libri Plureos GmbH in Hamburg,
Germany